SCHOOL HANDBOOKS:

SOME LEGAL CONSIDERATIONS

by
Mary Angela Shaughnessy, SCN, Ph.D.

Department of Elementary Schools
National Catholic Educational Association
ISBN #1-55833-022-4

TABLE OF CONTENTS

PREFACE

With the complexities of today's educational world, handbooks for students and parents, for teachers and for school board memebers have attempted to give greater specificity to the role that each of these parties plays. Questions arise as to what should be placed in such handbooks. This publication attempts to answer these questions.

A greater number of questions arise which deal with the legal implications of what is written in such handbooks. How binding are these documents? If something is omitted, is the school culpable? Must the books deal with every situation? What efforts must the school make to insure the information reaches those for whom it is intended? This publication also addresses such questions.

In addressing these questions, the author, Sister Angela Shaughnessy, S.C.N., Ph. D., places them within the framework of how law and state and federal regulations affect Catholic (private) schools. While some readers may be tempted to skip the first chapter and jump right into the practical aspects of the book, these readers will not truly understand the reason for many of the principles presented in later chapters. The first chapter presents a solid foundation for all that is to come.

The following three chapters which deal specifically with handbooks for faculty, parents and students, and members of the boards of education contain lists of items that should be in such handbooks, some consideration about the legal implications of what is said about each item and some suggestions on wording that might be used. An extensive glossary follows.

The Department of Elementary Schools is pleased to present this publication to the NCEA community. Writers of handbooks will find the comprehensive treatment helpful. The readable nature of the publication will make the work of the handbook developer easy. The many practical suggestions presented in this publication will further ease the task of such writers.

The Department expresses its gratitude to the author for this valuable publication which is both a tool for developing handbooks on the local level and a book that provides a framework for legal matters affecting Catholic schools.

August 1, 1989

Bonnie Pryor   **Robert J. Kealey**, F.S.C., Ed.D.
President   Executive Director

Department of Elementary Schools
National Catholic Educational Association

ABOUT THE AUTHOR

Sister Mary Angela Shaughnessy, S.C.N., Ph.D., is a member of the Sisters of Charity of Nazareth, Kentucky, who has taught at all levels of education and served as a principal of a Catholic school for eight years. Sister received her Bachelor of Arts degree from Spalding University, Louisville. She holds master's degrees in English from University of Louisville and in educational administration from Spalding. In 1985 she received her doctorate from Boston College in educational administration and supervision. Her dissertation is entitled *Student and Teacher Rights in Private Schools: Legal Cnsiderations for the Administrator.* Currently she is an Assistant Professor at Spalding University and has served as an adjunct professor at several other institutions. In 1988 she authored for NCEA *A Primer on School Law: A Guide for Board Members in Catholic Schools.*

INTRODUCTION

One of the more formidable tasks facing any Catholic school administrator is developing and writing school handbooks, those definitive references containing policies and procedures for which school community members are responsible.

Since school administrators are forced to be concerned with the legality of their actions and of their schools' policies, the importance of handbooks is paramount.

Administrators generally know that handbooks are significant. Catholic school administrators are accountable, in certain areas, to state educational authorities who are themselves governed by—and who govern by—state statutes and regulations. In addition, administrators in Catholic schools must answer to pastors in parish schools, to governing bodies of religious congregations if the school is sponsored by a religious congregation, and often to boards of directors and trustees. Administrators are accountable to parents for the educational experiences given their children and for the competence of the school personnel affording those experiences. Administrators are expected to give faculty and staff clear directions and to provide personnel policies that are just. Finally, administrators must always be concerned with both the legality and the morality of their actions.

Although the law is not the same in the public and private sectors, Catholic school administrators need some understanding of the evolution of school law in the public sector. Court decisions can offer guidance for Catholic school administrators seeking to develop legally sound and morally just policies and procedures. A brief mention of significant public sector cases is in order.

The last twenty years have witnessed a dramatic increase in the numbers and kinds of lawsuits brought against schools in general. Prior to the 1960s, very few cases involving parents, students, and/or teachers resulted in findings against the school.

The few cases which were brought were generally

decided in favor of the school since judges practiced the doctrine of judicial restraint, a belief which basically means that courts will not interfere in decisions made by professionals, unless blatantly unfair action has been taken. While that doctrine is still practiced today, judges seem to be somewhat more willing to decide against the school, particularly in the area of discipline.

A landmark college case which set the stage for many education cases, *Dixon v. Alabama State Board of Education* 294 F. 2d 150, cert. denied 368 U.S. 930 (1961), involved students who were suspended from school for taking part in a lunch counter sit-in. The justices ruled that students in public colleges and universities had a right to procedural due process. College administrators could no longer arbitrarily dismiss students or teachers at will. The accused had to be given a minimum of due process. Steps in due process include: (1) *notice*, the person is told what it is he or she is alleged to have done; (2) *hearing*, the person is given an opportunity to present his or her side of the story; (3) *before an impartial tribunal*, and the law assumes that a college or university official will be an impartial party. Thus, the court reasoned that education in a state university is a property interest. The court did not require a full-scale hearing for the students, but it did require that the basic elements of due process be met: *notice* and a *hearing* before an *impartial tribunal*.

After the *Dixon* case, many similar elementary and secondary cases were litigated. Three of these are particularly significant. *Tinker v. Des Moines Independent Community School District et al.* 393 U.S. 503 (1969) produced the now famous statement, "It can hardly be argued that either students or teachers shed their constitutional rights to freedom of speech or expression at the schoolhouse gate" (p. 506). Although this case involving students who were suspended from public elementary and secondary schools for wearing black armbands to protest the Vietnam War is rightfully associated with First Amendment freedom of speech rights, it is very significant in Fourteenth Amendment due process considerations as well. In the public sector, First Amendment rights cannot be restricted without due process of law.

A second landmark public school case, *Goss v. Lopez* 419

U.S. 565 (1974), involved Ohio public school students who, without a hearing, had been suspended from school for up to ten days. The Supreme Court ruled that suspended public school students do have rights to at least minimal due process protections. In an opinion that might provide food for thought for any administrator, public or private, the court stated:

> In holding as we do, we do not believe that we have imposed procedures on school disciplinarians which are inappropriate in a classroom setting. Instead we have imposed requirements which are, if anything, less than a fairminded principal would impose upon himself in order to avoid unfair suspensions (p. 583).

The *Goss* court called for actions based on a moral viewpoint, a sense of fair play, as much as on what the Constitution does and does not require. Courts rely on an expectation that educators are trying to do the right and honorable thing. Since educators are supposed to be modeling appropriate behaviors for students, courts will hold educators to strict standards of "fair play" where student misconduct is alleged.

In a second case heard the same day as *Goss, Wood v. Strickland*, 420 U.S. 308 (1974), the court ruled that school officials could be held liable for damages if their actions violated the rights of students. By 1974, then, the rights of public school students and teachers appeared to be firmly established. Even though some Supreme Court cases in the last three years show a somewhat more conservative interpretation of the rights of public school students, the right to due process has remained largely unchallenged.

Private schools are expected to be fair in their dealings with students and teachers, but that fairness is judged by the provisions of the contract existing between the school and the student or teacher. No constitutional due process protections exist in Catholic schools. Because the Catholic school is not an extension of the state, students and teachers cannot generally claim constitutional protections.

This lack of constitutional safeguards does not mean that Catholic schools may be arbitrary in their dealings with parents, students, and teachers, but it *does* mean that the Catholic school does not have to accept all the behaviors that the public school has no choice but to accept.

While the public school administrator has a fairly large body of case law available to help in understanding the rights of students, parents, and teachers in public schools, the Catholic school administrator has no comparable guide.

The last fifteen years, however, have seen a rise in the number of cases brought by Catholic school students, parents, and teachers. The reticence that once seemed to preclude a church member's suing a church authority has largely disappeared. In the past, the doctrine of separation of church and state has protected church sponsored schools from being successfully sued. Recent decisions suggest that that doctrine does not offer a church-related institution absolute protection from successful lawsuits.

A small but growing body of case law is emerging in the area of private (and, therefore, Catholic) school law. The fact that only one private school case, *Rendell-Baker v. Kohn* (1982) has reached the United States Supreme Court and the Court failed to find for the teacher, may indicate the reluctance of the high court to intervene in private education. The strong dissent in *Rendell-Baker*, along with the decisions coming from state and circuit courts, however, suggests that private school law is in a state of flux. The next several years should prove most crucial in the development of case law for the private and, therefore, Catholic school.

There are few legal resources available to the Catholic school administrator. Three NCEA publications should prove helpful: Steve Permuth, *et al. The Law, the Student and the Catholic School* (1981); Mary Angela Shaughnessy, *School Law Primer: A Guide for Board Members in Catholic Schools* (1988). In addition, the NCEA publishes *The Private School Law Digest* edited by Mary Agnes Lentz.

The study of the law as it impacts Catholic schools is relatively new and is one that needs development so that administrators of Catholic schools can be more knowledgeable about the rights of students and teachers in their institutions and more cognizant of their own responsibilities to protect those rights.

Catholic school administrators, concerned with both the duty to act justly and with the desire to avoid lawsuits, are wise to seek guidance in the writing of documents, particularly handbooks. Thus, the purpose of this book is to provide an introduction to the laws affecting the administration of Catholic schools as well as to offer specific advice on the content and wording of faculty, parent/student, and board handbooks.

THE LAWS AFFECTING CATHOLIC EDUCATION IN THE UNITED STATES

T he laws affecting education in the United States today can generally be classified according to four categories: (1) constitutional law (both state and federal); (2) administrative law: statutes and regulations; (3) common law principles; and (4) contract law. It must be kept in mind from the outset that public school law and nonpublic school law (in this case, Catholic school) differ greatly in many respects, primarily because the two school systems evolved from opposite sources.

Constitutional Law

Federal constitutional law

Federal constitutional law protects individuals against the arbitrary deprivation of their constitutional freedoms by government and government officials. Students and teachers in public schools are protected by constitutional law since public schools are governmental agencies and the administrators of public schools are public officials. Students and teachers in nonpublic schools are not protected by federal constitutional law because private schools are private agencies. When a student enrolls in a Catholic school, that student and/or the parents voluntarily surrender certain constitutional protections while in the Catholic school. Of course, a person in a private institution can always voluntarily leave that institution and enter the public sector where constitutional rights are protected, but as long as the person remains in the private sector, the Constitution offers no protection.

Therefore, what cannot lawfully be done in a public school may be done in a Catholic school, e.g., the First Amendment to the Constitution protects an individual's right to free speech. Therefore, administrators in public schools may not make rules prohibiting the expression of unpopular viewpoints. Since no such constitutional protection exists in the Catholic school, administrators may restrict the speech of both students and teachers.

State constitutional law

On the other hand, however, state constitutional law may apply to private as well as public schools. It is not unusual to find a statement such as, "Anyone operating an educational institution in this state shall be required to . . . ." So long as whatever is required does not unfairly impinge upon the rights of the private educational institution and can be shown to have some legitimate educational purpose, private schools can be compelled to comply with the state constitutional requirements which normally are not as restrictive as those of the federal Constitution.

Mix of federal and state constitutional law

The only situation in which a private school can be required to grant federal constitutional protections is if state action can be found to be so pervasive within the school that the school can fairly be said to be acting as an agent of an individual state. State action can be defined as:

> In general, term used in connection with claims under due process clause and Civil Rights Act for which a private citizen is seeking damages or redress because of improper governmental intrusion into his life. In determining whether an action complained of consti-

tutes "state action" within the purview of the Fourteenth Amendment, court must determine whether sufficiently close nexus exists between state and challenged action so that the action may fairly be treated as that of the state itself (Black, p. 1262).

Therefore, if state action can be demonstrated to exist in an institution or a specific program or activity of an institution, constitutional protections (of which due process is a major one) must be provided.

As Black's definition points out, the factor which determines the existence of state action is the nexus (relationship) between the state and the challenged action.

Given that nonpublic schools have the right to exist, *Pierce v. Society of Sisters (1925)*, and since they are not bound to grant constitutional protections, unless significant state action is found, litigants alleging a denial of constitutional rights will have to prove the existence of significant state action within the institution before the court will grant relief. It is very important for Catholic school officials to keep these facts in mind. It is not uncommon for parents, students, or teachers to claim that their federal constitutional rights have been violated in the Catholic school when, in fact, no constitutional rights ever existed.

Some of the main arguments advanced to prove the presence of state action in private educational institutions are: (1) an institution's acceptance of government monies; (2) the tax- exempt status of the private institution; (3) education as a quasi state function (sometimes called a "public benefit theory" since schools, particularly elementary and secondary ones, perform a public service); and (4) state involvement with the school through accreditation or similar procedures and/or statutory requirements with which the school complies.

Three nonpublic school cases (one from a non-sectarian school and two from Catholic schools) are examples of cases in which private school students advanced "state action" arguments which, if accepted by the courts, would have entitled them to the protections of the federal Constitution.

A 1970 Indiana case, *Bright v. Isenbarger* 314 F. Supp. 1382, involved two high school sophomores suspended for the duration of the school year from a Catholic school for violation of a rule. The dismissed students alleged state action because of the following factors: the state regulated the educational standards of private schools; the state granted private schools tax-exempt status; and the school received some state and federal aid. The court rejected the plaintiffs' arguments and stated that no significant state action was present. Further, the court held that even if significant state action had been found, it would have to be substantially involved in the contested activity, for example, the expulsion or the disciplinary code. The court concluded:

> Not only do plaintiffs fail to have any compelling judicial support for their contentions but they have invited this court to adopt a rationale of decision which would effectively eliminate private education . . . . A decision which would encompass such a result raises questions of profound constitutional significance, since the right of parents to maintain and of children to attend private schools is among their fundamental personal liberties and enriches our highly valued tradition of social pluralism. . . . Yet the fact that the State provides tuition-free schools in order to promote an educated citizenry does not mean that *all private* educational institutions perform a "public function" (pp. 1397-98).

The *Bright* court definitively rejected the "public benefit" theory as it applies to the Catholic school. One cannot conclude that private schools perform a public function because they perform a public service.

In the second significant case, *Geraci v. St. Xavier High School* Ohio Opinions 13 3d 146 (1978), a student who had been expelled for encouraging someone to throw a pie in the face of a teacher, sought to invoke the state action argument. The plaintiff alleged that state action was present and that he was entitled to constitutional protections, the same way a student in a public high school would be. The court sought to determine whether a "symbiotic relationship" (cf. Black's "nexus") existed between the state and the administration and operation of the school such that state action could be proven to exist. Earlier public school decisions (cf. *Goss v. Lopez* 419 U.S. 565, 1975) clearly stated that public education was a right extended by the state, and, therefore, state action was present in the conduct of public school officials; in *Geraci*, the court had to determine whether state action could possibly be construed as being present in any of the school's operations. The court did not find a symbiotic relationship, nor any other type of state action present in the school and ruled that private schools are not bound by due process considerations as required by the federal Constitution. However, the court did indicate that courts could intervene in the disciplinary proceedings of private schools:

> A private school's disciplinary proceedings are not controlled by the due process clause, and accordingly such schools have broad discretion in making rules and setting up procedures for their enforcement, nevertheless, under its broad equitable powers a court will intervene where such discretion is abused or the proceedings do not comport with fundamental fairness (pp. 149-50).

This court suggests that, even if state action does not exist in private schools, the schools may still be held to a standard of "fundamental fairness." This phrase is sometimes used as a synonym for due process, although constitutional due process requires specific protections as laid down in the law and interpreted by the courts. Fundamental fairness in a Catholic school, though akin to constitutional due process, is not to be equated with it.

In a case similar to *Geraci* in 1976 in Delaware, *Wisch v. Sanford School, Inc.* 420 F. Supp. 1310, a student was

5

expelled for using marijuana. The student argued that the presence of federal funds in a private school constituted state action, thus requiring that constitutional protections apply. The federal funding took the following forms: transportation subsidies; National School Lunch Program aid; ESEA funds; a part-time driver education instructor salary; and a federal grant for a radio station. The court rejected the argument that the above forms constituted state action. However, the court did scrutinize the school's rules and the dissemination of the code of conduct to determine that contractual, procedural fairness had been given the plaintiff. The court specifically addressed the basic fairness provision in a private school-student relationship and stated that such a provision would have been better met by a written disciplinary code. While the courts do not tend to find state action present in private schools, they are looking for some kind of fairness, as the above cases demonstrate.

The private school cases just cited indicate that, without a finding of significant state action in a private school or an activity, the courts will not hold private school administrators to the requirements of constitutional protections. The case law should not be interpreted to mean that private schools and their administrators can do anything they wish to students and the courts will not intervene because of the absence of state action. Case law is constantly being developed, and so it is difficult to lay down hard and fast rules. No case involving student discipline in a private school has ever reached the Supreme Court. In a 1982 case, *Rendell-Baker v. Kohn*, 102 S.Ct. 2764, which involved a teacher dismissed from a private school that received over 95% of its funding from the government, the Supreme Court declined to find state action. The Court, however, ruled instead that the state would have had to be involved in the contested activity (in this case, the dismissal), before state action would be found to be present to such a degree that the protections of the Constitution could be invoked.

The above discussion emphasizes, however, that while courts may not be willing to accept the state action argument in cases involving student and teacher rights, they do look for the presence of fairness in a school's dealings with students and teachers.

In any consideration of fairness in the private sector, some discussion of due process in the public sector is in order. Almost all cases concerning student and teacher rights in public schools involve the legal concept of due process. Although constitutional due process is required in the public schools and not in the nonpublic schools, administrators may find knowledge of due process and its implications helpful in the development and implementation of rules, procedures, and policies. Some historical background concerning due process is necessary if administrators are to develop policies which are legally and morally defensible.

Due Process

The democratic principle of due process has its basis in the theory of social contract. Plato was among the first to articulate this theory which was substantially developed in modern times by Locke and Rousseau: "The justification for the state's existence, according to Locke, was based on its ability to protect those rights better than individuals could on their own" (LaMorte, 1977, p. 32). Locke's ideas are reflected in the Declaration of Independence which guarantees "certain inalienable rights, among these are life, liberty and pursuit of happiness." The Fifth Amendment to the Constitution guarantees that no person shall "be deprived of life, liberty or property, without due process of law." The Fourteenth Amendment extends that guarantee to the actions of individual states and protects the citizen against arbitrary state action: "No state shall make or enforce any law which shall abridge the privileges or immunities of the citizens of the United States; nor shall any State deprive any person of life, liberty or property, without due process of law"(Amendment XIV, Section 1, *The Constitution of the United States*, adopted 1868).

The Civil Rights Act of 1871 protects persons whose individual constitutional rights are denied by state authorities.

The Civil Rights Act applies to persons acting—or upon the receiving end of actions "under color of state law" (15 *American Jurisprudence* 2d 415). The actions of private individuals who are not in some way functioning as agents of the state are not governed by the Civil Rights Act or by the provisions of the Fifth and Fourteenth Amendments.

Therefore, Catholic schools generally cannot be legally required to provide constitutional due process protections unless state action can be found in the school or unless such protections are guaranteed by contract. Nonetheless, Catholic schools should develop and act upon a due process model which, while not a constitutional one, is one that protects the rights of individuals in the light of the Gospel and church documents.

Although much has been written about due process, one of its simplest definitions is simply "fairness." Persons expect that parties to a suit in court will be treated fairly by the judge and/or the jury: anyone accused of a crime will be told what it is that person is alleged to have done (notice); he or she will be given a hearing or trial by an impartial party; the accused will be able to confront the accusers (cross-examination) and call witnesses. These expectations have been defined as "procedural due process."

Kern Alexander (1980) has discussed procedural due process as "if an individual is to be deprived of his life, liberty or property, a prescribed constitutional procedure must be followed" (p. 343).

Procedural due process has also been discussed by way of questions: What process is due? What procedures are followed? Are they reasonable? Are all persons treated fairly and, insofar as possible, in the same way? Are there clear procedures that persons can expect will be followed?

Traditionally, the courts have held that there are two types of due process: procedural and substantive. The concept of substantive due process is somewhat more difficult to understand than is the concept of procedural due process. Its root word, *substance*, might be helpful in understanding the concept. A person cannot violate

—

someone's substantive due process rights unless the "substance" of which one is to be deprived is one to which the individual has an existing right in the first place.

Kern Alexander (1980, p. 343) has discussed substantive due process as follows: "If a state is going to deprive a person of his life, liberty or property, the state must have a valid objective and the means used must be reasonably calculated to achieve the objective." Substantive due process can also be defined as fundamental reasonableness or fairness (the reasonableness or fairness that public schools must provide is found in the Constitution). Substantive due process involves moral as well as legal ramifications: is this action fair and reasonable? Substantive due process applies wherever *property* or *liberty* interests can be demonstrated.

Property interest has been defined as "everything which is or may be the subject of ownership, whether [it is] a legal ownership . . . or a private ownership" (Black, 1979, p. 1095). A person's tangible property constitutes a property interest. In the public sector, the right to an education in government- maintained schools is a property interest guaranteed by the state. But certain conditions must be met before a property interest, such as tenure, can be advanced.

Although persons in Catholic institutions may not have constitutional protection of their property rights (e.g. a teacher's employment contract, a parent's assurance that a child is being educated, and/or the child's right to learn in a safe environment), such persons do have property protections founded in law. The Supreme Court in *Board of Regents v. Roth* 408 U.S. 564, 92 S. Ct. 2701 (1972), involving the non-renewal of a one-year teaching contract of a first-year professor, declared:

> To have a property interest in a benefit, a person clearly must have more than an abstract need or desire for it. He must have more than a unilateral expectation of it. He must, instead, have a legitimate claim of entitlement to it.
>
> It is a purpose of the ancient institution of property to protect those claims upon which people rely in their daily lives. . . (p. 577).

This statement is important to keep in mind when one begins to consider the rights of students and teachers in private schools and the responsibilities of private school administrators in protecting those rights. The *Roth* case provides further direction for the private (as well as the public) school administrator who might be tempted to think that, if a right cannot be found in the federal Constitution, one need not be too concerned with its protection. In *Roth* the court clearly stated that the Constitution does not create property interests; such interests are created and governed by the independent and separate entity which can be considered the source of the interests, such as state law or contract law. Contract law, which is the main source of the law for Catholic schools, thus may require Catholic schools to grant some degree of due process to persons in those schools.

The above- cited *Roth* case indicated that a person has to be able to claim a particular right before the court can uphold that right and before any administrator can be held responsible for protecting it. The court clearly stated that tenure has to be achieved according to the regulations established by whatever body is charged with the responsibility for developing those standards. A person must be entitled to tenure before he or she can claim a right to re-employment. The court in *Roth* held that without a clear right to tenure, a property interest, the employee could not enlist the court's aid simply because of a wish to be re-employed.

The *Roth* court found that no constitutional right to due process existed because the instructor had no property interest in the renewal of his contract, which was clearly a one-year contract, and because the court could find no violation of a liberty interest (a person's interest in or right to reputation).

If the instructor had been able to prove damage to reputation, then, the court indicates, a different decision might have been reached.

The *Roth* case provides a clear example of lack of property interest and demonstrates the possible outcome of any lawsuit brought by a teacher who had been employed in any school system (public or private) for a period of time less than that required for tenure. The longer the teacher has been employed by a school, the more difficult it is to dismiss the teacher, as the following case illustrates.

In a situation somewhat similar to *Roth, Perry v. Sindermann* 408 U.S. 593 (1972), the court found for the teacher because the teacher had been employed for ten years. Thus, the court reasoned that an expectation of continuing employment had been created and that the instructor had a property interest in re-employment.

Tenure has been defined as an expectation of continuing employment. In the Catholic school system, it is rare to find a written policy regarding tenure. Some Catholic school administrators maintain that everyone is on a year-to-year contract and that anyone can be dismissed at the end of the school year. The *Sinderman* case indicates that such an assumption may be false. Some courts discuss a concept called *de facto* tenure (tenure in fact). In *Sinderman*, the court ruled that the school had created an expectation of continuing employment by employing the instructor for ten years and therefore, the teacher had tenure in fact. It would thus seem that Catholic schools could find themselves in the position of having created *de facto* tenure situations.

Although Catholic schools are not required to follow constitutional due process procedures, these and other nonpublic schools can learn much from cases alleging deprivation of constitutional rights in the public school.

It would seem that the Judaeo/Christian ethic requires that at least the rudiments of due process be afforded persons in Catholic institutions. Granting a minimum of due process would not only meet the demands of the Gospel, but it would also help to insure that Catholic schools are acting in a wise and ethical manner.

Administrative Law: Statutes and Regulations

Administrative law, which encompasses federal and state statutes and regulations, governs the public school and may govern the private school as well. Failure to comply with reasonable regulations can result in the imposition of sanctions. The relatively recent case of *Bob Jones University v. United States* 103 S. Ct. 2017 (1983) illustrates this point. When Bob Jones University, a nonpublic institution, was found to use racially discriminatory admissions policies, the Internal Revenue Service withdrew the university's tax-exempt status based on a 1970 regulation proscribing the granting of tax-exempt status to any institution which discriminated on the basis of race. Before a private school will be forced to comply with a law or regulation, the state will have to demonstrate a *compelling interest* in the enforcement of the regulation. Black (1979) defines compelling state interest as a: "Term used to uphold state action in the face of attack, grounded on Equal Protection or First Amendment rights because of serious need for such state action" (p. 256).

In the *Bob Jones* case, the government's compelling interest in racial equality was sufficient for the court to order Bob Jones University to comply with the anti-discrimination regulation or lose its tax-exempt status.

Other examples of compelling state interests in educational concerns might be curriculum or graduation requirements, teacher certification and school certification regulations. In these cases the state could very possibly prove a compelling state interest in the proper education of the public.

The state cannot pass laws so restrictive that a school's existence is placed in jeopardy. The right of the private school to exist was firmly established by the Supreme Court in 1925 when two agencies operating private schools brought suit challenging an Oregon statute which would have made public education compulsory. In this landmark case, *Pierce v. the Society of Sisters* 268 U.S. 510 (1925), the Supreme Court declared the statute unconstitutional not only because it interfered with the rights of the school owners, but also because it interfered with the right of parents to choose the education of their children.

Common Law

The third type of law which applies to both the public and private sectors (and, indeed, to all cases, whether school cases or not) is the common law. *Black's Law Dictionary* (1979) defines common law:

> As distinguished from law created by the enactment of legislatures, the common law comprises the body of those principles and rules of action, relating to the government and security of persons and property, which derive their authority solely from the usages and customs of immemorial, antiquity, or from the judgments and decrees of the courts recognizing, affirming, and enforcing such usages and customs; ... "Common law" consists of those principles, usage and rules of action applicable to government and security of persons and property which do not rest for their authority upon any express and positive declaration of the will of the legislature (p. 251).

Sometimes called judge-made law, common law principles may also be considered to be derived from God's law, especially by persons in religious schools. Many common law principles are founded in basic morality, such as that contained in the Bible. Therefore, it is not uncommon for a court to discuss basic fairness or common law standards of decency in a decision, even without reference to a specific state or federal law.

Contract Law

The fourth kind of law which governs both public and private schools is contract law. Public schools are governed by contract law in some instances, especially in the area of teacher contracts. However, most cases involving public school teacher contracts also allege violation of constitutionally protected interests as well, so contract law is not the only applicable law.

In the nonpublic school and, therefore, in the Catholic school, contract law is the predominant governing law. A contract may be defined as: "An agreement between two or more persons which creates an obligation to do or not to do a particular thing" (Black, 1979, pp. 291-92).

Generally, the five basic elements of a contract are: (1) mutual assent (2) by legally competent parties for (3) consideration (4) to subject matter that is legal and (5) in a form of agreement which is legal.

Mutual assent implies that two parties entering into a contract agree to its provisions. A Catholic school agrees to provide an education to a student, and the parents accept that arrangement, or a Catholic school offers a teacher a contract which the teacher accepts. "To be binding a contract must have both a legal 'offer' and 'acceptance'" (Mawdsley and Permuth, unpublished manuscript, p. 5).

Consideration is what the first party agrees to do for the other party in exchange for something from the second party. The private school agrees to provide educational services to a student in return for payment of tuition and adherence to school rules. The school agrees to pay the teacher a salary in return for teaching services.

Legally competent parties implies that the parties entering into the contract are lawfully qualified to make the agreement. A school is legally qualified to enter into contracts to educate students and to employ teachers. Parents are legally competent to agree to pay tuition and meet other obligations (minor students are not legally competent, and so parents or legal guardians must sign contracts on their behalf). A properly qualified teacher is a legally competent party; a person who does not possess the qualifications or skills needed to perform as a teacher would not be a legally competent party to enter into a teaching contract.

Legal subject matter assumes that the provisions of the contract are legal. An agreement that a teacher would not marry a person of another race as a condition of employment might not be legal, as such a condition would probably be construed as a violation of anti-discrimination laws.

Legal form may vary from state to state. If a contract calls for witnesses and no witnesses' signatures are found on the contract, then the contract is probably not in proper legal form. If any one of the five elements of a contract is missing, the contract may be held to be null and void.

Cases involving student and teacher discipline (particularly, dismissal) in Catholic schools often allege breach of contract:

> A breach of contract occurs when a party does not perform that which he or she was under an absolute duty to perform and the circumstances are such that his or her failure was neither justified nor excused (Gatti and Gatti, 1983, p. 24).

Breach of contract can be committed by either party to the contract (the school/administrator or the teacher or student). It is generally conceded, however, that it is futile for a school to seek to bring breach of contract charges against a teacher who wants to terminate a contract; it is highly unlikely that a judge will compel a person to teach against his or her wishes. Historically, courts will not compel performance of a contract, since a contractual arrangement is seen as a private arrangement, and courts will not force persons to associate with each other against their will. The remedy for breach of contract is damages. In order for a school to collect damages, it would have to show that it had been damaged. Generally, a court will rule that it is not very difficult to replace a teacher, and so damages are not appropriate.

While teachers can usually break their contracts without severe consequences, schools and administrators who terminate a teacher's employment during a contract term without just cause or who terminate a student's enrollment without just cause can ordinarily expect to pay damages if a lawsuit is filed. Two cases involving breach of contract in Catholic schools will illustrate the concept.

In the breach of contract case of a teacher in a Roman Catholic school, *Weithoff v. St. Veronica School* 210 N.W. 2d 108 Michigan, (1973), the court concerned itself with the case of a woman who had been dismissed from her position because of her marriage to an ex-priest. The court was careful to note that a church-sponsored school could contractually require teachers and other employees to observe the tenets of its faith. The testimony shows that a new regulation requiring teachers to be practicing Catholics had been adopted by the school board but had never been promulgated. Therefore, the court held that the school could not legally dismiss the teacher without being liable for damages. Obviously, if the principal and/or school board had been careful to disseminate its regulations, this case might have had a different ending.

An opposite conclusion was reached in the similar case of *Steeber v. Benilde-St. Margaret's High School* No. D.C. 739 378, Hennepin County, Minnesota, (1978) in which a teacher protested the non-renewal of her contract following her remarriage after a civil divorce. The court upheld the right of the school to terminate the teacher's contract since she was no longer a member in good standing of the Catholic church.

In the first case, the school breached its contract with the teacher because it failed to promulgate the rule to which it sought to hold the teacher. In the second case, though, in a very similar situation, the court ruled in the school's favor because the school had properly proceeded according to its contract.

William D. Valente (1980) offers this advice to teachers in private schools who think that their rights are being violated:

> Thus, a teacher who is offended by private school orders that suppress speech, invade privacy, or impose disciplinary sanctions without notice or hearing must look else where than to constitutional doctrines for legal relief, except in the unusual situation where the private school is considered to be engaged in official government action (p. 464).

The "elsewhere" to which a Catholic school teacher must look is, generally, contract law. Mr. Valente's words are a timely admonition to faculty in Catholic schools as they consider their rights and responsibilities and to administrators as they develop, revise and implement contracts and handbooks.

The relationship of both public and private institutions to students has been compared to that of a fiduciary. Professor Warren Seavey first applied this theory to public institutions in 1957, three years before the landmark *Dixon* case. Seavey maintained that because an educational institution was subject to the duties of a fiduciary in dealing with its students, it should at least have to explain to students what rights they are waiving when they (or their parents) sign a form. Writing in the *Harvard Law Review*, Professor Seavey takes a strong stand:

> It is shocking that the officials of a state educational institution, which can function properly only if our freedoms are preserved, should not understand the elementary principles of fair play. It is equally shocking to find that a court support them in denying to a student the protection given to a pickpocket (p. 1407).

"The protection given to a pickpocket" became an oft-quoted phrase and illustrated the apparent injustice in giving more protections to common criminals than to students. A little more than a decade later, Professor Charles Wright (1969), in the *Vanderbilt Law Review*, would seem to apply Professor Seavey's sentiments to the private sector:

> [It] seems. . .unthinkable. . . that the faculty and administration of any private institution would consider recognizing fewer rights in their students than the minimum the Constitution exacts of the state universities, or that their students would long remain quiescent if a private college were to embark on such a benighted course (pp. 1027, 35).

A fiduciary is charged with showing that whatever is done is done honestly. This approach would shift the burden of proof from the student to the institution. One can see elements of the common law and fundamental fairness arguments here. A reasonable individual would expect that a person or institution charged with the care of others would exercise that care or be able to show just cause why the care was not given; thus, one might expect the same of an institution charged with imparting learning. Critics of such an approach may raise any of several objections but the theory itself is worthy of administrative consideration and is one that has been cited by the courts.

The evolution that has occurred since Seavey's and Wright's statements might contain a lesson for nonpublic school administrators. The day may not be far off when courts will require due process protections from private school administrators; if the justification for such action cannot legitimately be found in the Constitution, the courts may find it in contract law or statutory requirements.

Duties of Principals and Teachers

Principals

Principals generally have numerous duties and responsibilities, many of which are not clearly defined in any document. The safest course might be for a principal to assume that he or she is responsible for everything in the school. (In a parish school, of course, the pastor would have the ultimate authority, as canon law dictates). The principal may delegate decision-making powers to other persons, but the responsibility cannot be delegated. If a lawsuit were to be brought against a school and/or a teacher, it is virtually certain that the principal would be sued as well.

Principals' duties can be summarized under two headings:

(1) policy formation and communication of rules and policies and,

(2) supervision of teachers and other personnel. Almost every activity a principal does can be placed under one of these two categories.

Even though school boards and pastors may have the final responsibility for ultimately approving policy, the principal should play a crucial role in developing it. It is hard to imagine a Catholic school board's writing and approving policy without seeking the principal's input. The best models for policy development are ones that either have the principal write the first draft of the policy and bring it to the board or a committee for discussion and revision or have the principal serve as a member of a committee developing policy in a given area or areas. It is important that both pastor and board recognize the principal as the educational expert in the school and utilize that expertise to the fullest extent possible. Principals also communicate policy and provide for its implementation.

One of the principal's most serious responsibilities is the supervision of teachers. It is crucial that administrators, teachers, and board members understand that the supervision and evaluation of teachers are the principal's responsibility. The principal is supposed to insure that the best possible educational experience is given to students. In reality, supervision is quality control for the school.

Supervision of personnel is not just determining that persons are performing their tasks in a satisfactory manner; it is also job protection for the teacher. If a principal does not supervise a teacher, and allegations are later made against the teacher, the principal will have no evidence to use in support of the teacher. If a teacher is faced with a malpractice suit charging failure to teach or inadequate teaching, the principal is the person best-equipped to assist the teacher in meeting those charges. One would hope that the principal's supervisory data show that the teacher was doing an adequate job in the classroom.

Teachers

The duties of teachers can also be classified under two headings: (1) implementing school rules and policies and (2) supervising the safety and learning of students.

It is important that teachers understand that their job is to implement rules, even if they do not personally agree with them. Lack of agreement is not a reason to fail to enforce a rule. If a teacher cannot support a given rule or policy, that teacher can use whatever channels exist to modify the rule, but until a change is made, the teacher is obligated to follow the directive. If a person cannot, in conscience, support the action required and change cannot be effected, then that person's only real choice is to leave the situation and seek other employment.

Supervision of children's safety and learning has both mental and physical implications. It is not enough for a teacher to be bodily present; the teacher must concentrate on the students. There have been a number of student accidents and injuries that could have been avoided if the teacher had been paying closer attention to the students. The concepts of mental and physical supervision will be discussed in greater detail in the last chapter.

The following chapters will deal with faculty, parent/ student and board handbooks. The last chapter will discuss some specific areas of tort liability concern.

FACULTY HANDBOOKS

The development and/or revision of a faculty handbook may well be one of the most important responsibilities facing an administrator. Administrators and teachers can much more easily know what is expected of them if all policies and pertinent information are gathered into one document.

New administrators may find themselves in a situation in which no handbook exists or in which the existing handbook is very incomplete or seemingly inappropriate or even at odds with what the new administrator desires in the school.

Seasoned administrators may feel that their handbooks are inadequate and could stand improvement but may decide, consciously or not, that there are more important claims on their time.

So a new or veteran administrator may know that the school handbook needs revision but may be at a loss as to where to begin the process of developing or revising a handbook. The following pages will suggest areas that should be considered in the formulation of a legally sound faculty handbook for the Catholic school.

One helpful technique, keeping a series of index cards, may be employed over a period of time prior to the actual composition and dissemination of the handbook. Every time the administrator thinks of something that should be in the handbook, that item is written on an index card. The administrator may wish to enlist the help of the faculty and staff by asking them to submit similar index cards containing any items they believe should be included in the handbook. It is helpful to confine each card to one item only.

Later, the cards can be sorted by categories for inclusion in the handbook. Such an approach can help the administrator to understand that writing or revising the handbook can be accomplished in steps, rather than in a monumental one-time writing.

There is more than one approach to organizing the contents of a handbook. Some administrators prefer an alphabetical approach; such an approach certainly can make finding items in a handbook easier. However, an administrator could decide that a topical arrangement is more suitable to a given school's needs.

Exhibit I presents a Faculty Handbook Checklist. The administrator may want to copy this checklist and use it to make notes as this chapter is studied and/or as other suggestions or thoughts are presented. The checklist could be shared with faculty so that teacher input could be gathered.

EXHIBIT I FACULTY HANDBOOK CHECKLIST		
	What should a school have concerning?	What does my school need?
Philosophy		
Teaching Duties		
Non-teaching Duties		
Supervision of Teachers		
Personnel Policies		
Sample Forms		

School Philosophy

The school philosophy should be the basis for all policies and procedures. Ideally, the life of the school should be seen as flowing from the philosophy. Basically, the Catholic school philosophy answers the question, "What do we as Catholic educators say that we are doing in this school?"

Courts expect that the rules and regulations of a school will be consistent with the stated philosophy of the school. It is important, therefore, that the administrator review rules and proposed rule changes in the light of the philosophy.

Many schools have philosophies, and in those cases, it is a good idea to review the philosophy at least once a year in order to evaluate the school's performance against the philosophy. Areas of significant disagreement should be settled, so that each year the faculty and staff can "own" the philosophy and those policies and procedures which emanate from it.

What about schools that do not have philosophies? The administrator would be well advised to begin the process of developing a philosophy with the faculty and, so far as possible, the parents. Although the development and writing of a philosophy is not the purpose of this study, some points for philosophy development are suggested in the sample handbook outline at the end of this chapter.

The philosophy provides a gauge for determining policies and procedures and for measuring success in attaining them. It would be difficult to justify a policy that is clearly at odds with the philosophy of the school; furthermore, the philosophy should help in the development of all policies and procedures.

Teaching Duties

At first glance, it might appear that teaching duties should occupy the bulk of the handbook. Certainly, those duties are the ones that are uppermost in the minds of administrators writing or revising handbooks. There are at least three main areas of teaching duties.

Instruction of students

The first area might be entitled "Instruction of Students." Teachers should be clearly told what they are expected to do in the instruction of students. It is not necessary to dictate *how* teachers are to do everything, but it is necessary to delineate some broad guidelines as to *what* they are to accomplish.

For example, a handbook might contain some directives as to whether textbooks are to be "covered" in their entirety; there should be some designation of the persons to be consulted for help and direction (principal, department head, grade level coordinator, etc.). Appropriate methods of teaching might be discussed. Amounts of time given for seatwork or independent study should be indicated.

Minimum and maximum times for homework assignments should be stated.

Supervision of students

A second area might be called "Supervision of Students" within the learning situation. Supervision outside the regular classroom learning situation would be discussed under non-teaching duties.

The responsibilities of teachers for students in the classroom should be thoroughly discussed. The fact that supervision is mental (the person has to be paying attention to the students) as well as physical (the teacher is bodily present) should be stressed.

Procedures for leaving students unattended should be discussed. There are situations, such as emergencies, that could require a teacher to leave a classroom unattended. Courts recognize this fact; however, courts do expect that students will not be left without directions as to their behavior. The standard courts use is: the younger the children chronologically or mentally, the greater the standard of care. If a teacher must leave the students, what procedures should be followed? How should the teacher insure that students know what to do in the absence of a teacher?

Record-keeping/grading

A third area involving teaching duties would be that of "Grading and Record-keeping." The school should clearly state what factors are to be considered in the determination of grades. Letter grades and numerical equivalents should be defined.

Teachers should know what their responsibilities are in regard to record-keeping. How long should attendance records be kept? States have different requirements, but, at the minimum, attendance records should be kept for five years after the student graduates or leaves the school. There have been cases in which the police and courts have asked for the school to verify a student's attendance on a particular day, even several years after an alleged incident occurred. If it is possible to keep the attendance records indefinitely, a school should do so.

Teachers or the school office staff should keep grade books on file, in the event that a student challenges a grade or brings a lawsuit necessitating verification of a grade. Conflicts regarding grades can be avoided if there is a policy in place stating that any request for consideration of a grade change must be made within a given number of days after the reception of the report card.

Teachers should keep their plan books on file either in the school office or in their home in case an educational malpractice suit should be filed against them. The plan book will indicate that the teacher did follow the curriculum and did teach whatever concepts were required.

Professionalism

Teachers are professionals, and all educators need

to be periodically reminded of the expectations of the profession and of their duties to the institution which employs them. Hence, a principal may wish to include some statement about professionalism and loyalty in the faculty handbook.

Non-Teaching Duties

Non-teaching duties comprise a significant portion of teacher responsibility. An administrator might want to utilize the index card method and begin writing down everything a teacher is expected to do that is not, strictly speaking, an instructional duty. Even if the school has a handbook, an administrator might find that a week or so of keeping "non-teaching duties" in mind is a worthwhile exercise.

Cafeteria, playground, study hall supervision

Some non-teaching duties come immediately to mind. In the elementary school, teachers are very often assigned to supervise the playground and the cafeteria. What exactly is a playground supervisor supposed to do? If he or she is expected to be present on the playground from one bell to the next, that expectation should be stated in the handbook. Procedures for accidents and reporting fighting and/or other disciplinary problems should be included.

For teachers assigned to cafeteria or study hall supervision, the same types of questions should be answered. If teachers are not to leave the students they are supervising except in case of an emergency, then the handbook should state that rule.

Student discipline

Teachers are expected to enforce student discipline. The student disciplinary code should be included in the faculty handbook, even if it is printed in a separate handbook for parents and/or students, so that teachers have all policies and procedures readily accessible in one place. The disciplinary actions that are reserved to the principal or other administrative personnel should be outlined.

Field trip policies and procedures

The area of field trips has been largely problematic for schools, yet, almost all teachers would agree that field trips can be very worthwhile parts of the teaching/learning experience. All steps which should be followed before taking a field trip should be cited in detail.

Extra-curricular activities

Teachers are almost always expected to sponsor some sort of extra-curricular activity. These activities can range from candy drives and Christmas plays to coaching sports.

The faculty handbook should state the school's expectations regarding teacher sponsorship for extra-curricular activities. Can each teacher be required to moderate one or more activities? Will the more time-consuming activities carry compensation and, if so, what is the scale of compensation?

The responsibilities of extra-curricular moderators should be presented, perhaps in outline form. Activities such as dances might benefit from a checklist-type approach so that teachers can easily see if they have met their responsibilities.

Attendance at meetings and other school events

A final area of non-teaching duties consists of meetings. What meetings are teachers expected to attend? Parent/Teacher conferences? PTA meetings? School drama presentations? It might be helpful to publish a yearly list of meetings that teachers will be responsible for attending. Administrators might wish to reserve the right to require attendance at other meetings in the course of the year. Perhaps a statement that, as far as possible, a certain number of days' notice will be given, would be helpful.

Supervision and Evaluation of Teachers

Supervision and evaluation of teachers certainly involve matters of personnel policy. Since these activities are the most important for both faculty and administration, a separate section is devoted to their consideration.

Frequency and format

Administrators have a responsibility to supervise and evaluate teachers. But teachers have the right to know approximately how often they can expect to be supervised and what format the report of the supervisory visit will take. Therefore, "Supervision and Evaluation of Teachers" is a fourth area that should be included in faculty handbooks.

Supervision can be problematic for both the principal and the teacher. A principal who never taught any grade lower than the sixth may feel inadequate in a first grade teacher's classroom; a high school principal who taught English may feel less than competent in a physics classroom. However, administrators and all effective educators should be able to recognize good teaching within five to ten minutes after entering a classroom. If supervision is an ongoing, formative process, then both the principal and the teacher can grow together and help each other to improve the learning environment of the school. If supervision is seen as punitive—as something that is only engaged in if the principal is "out to get a teacher," then it will hardly be successful.

Evaluation is summative: an administrator sums up all the available data and makes a decision regarding contract renewal. Evaluation of teaching performance, then, should be based on more than supervisory data. A principal will seek to answer such questions as, "Does this teacher support the rules of the school?" "Does he or she look after the safety of the children?" as well as "Is he or she a good subject matter teacher?" Evaluation then is a more encompassing concept than supervision, but both should be present in a good school. The demands placed upon administrators make it too easy to defer supervision; to state that "I wish I could observe teachers' classrooms, but I just don't have time" or "Mrs. Smith probably isn't doing a very good job, but she is a nice person, and I don't have the heart to fire her. Besides, who needs the hassle anyway?" is unacceptable.

All school administrators must understand that teachers and administrators are in schools for the students; the students are not there for the teachers' employment. Surely, there is no more sacred responsibility than insuring that students are being taught by capable, competent, caring professionals and that all teachers are encouraged and given the means to become the best professionals they can be.

Ultimately, it is the principal who is responsible for the supervision and evaluation of teachers even if someone else, such as the pastor, signs the contract—because the principal is the chief executive officer of the school. Supervision and evaluation enable a principal to make wise decisions about contract renewal. It is not just for a principal to decide not to renew a teacher's contract if the principal has never observed the teacher at work. Unfortunately, most educators can recall one or more situations in which a person lost a teaching position because he or she couldn't keep order or was considered incompetent, even though the person's principal had never been in the classroom. Written observations that have been shared with the teachers involved provide some of the best data available in making employment decisions. A principal can use the data to ask questions at the end of the year. For example, "We have discussed some of the difficulties you have had with keeping the other children on task while you are working with the reading groups. I know that you have tried thus and such a strategy, and when I last visited your classroom, it seemed to be working fairly well. Have you tried any other strategies or had any other thoughts about how to better the learning environment for the students when your attention necessarily can't be on the total group?"

The handbook should state the school policy on supervision of teachers. Who is responsible for supervising teachers/visiting classrooms? Is it the principal's sole responsibility, or are other persons, such as vice-principals, department heads, or level coordinators, involved? How often will the teacher be supervised? What format will be used?

Scheduled vs. unscheduled visits

Will the supervisor's visits be scheduled or unscheduled? If the visits are normally scheduled (for example, twice a semester or three times a year), does the principal/other administrator reserve the right to observe classes at unscheduled times?

The teacher also has a right to know how he or she will be evaluated. How will the supervisory visits be incorporated into the end-of-the year evaluation? Who will see this evaluation? Will the evaluation become part of the teacher's permanent file? Does the teacher have an opportunity to respond in writing to the evaluation? Will the teacher's response become part of the evaluation record? Considering these questions and developing policies to answer them will help an administrator operate on fairly solid legal ground.

Although most educators would agree that supervision is a formative experience and evaluation is a summative one, the distinction becomes blurred in many Catholic schools where the principal serves as both supervisor and evaluator. These dual responsibilities can present very real problems. A teacher may be reluctant to discuss problems with a principal if he or she thinks that information could be used against him or her in an evaluation. Catholic school principals who wear both hats need to be especially knowledgeable of human relations and of sound legal practice.

Personnel Policies

The personnel policies of a school should be stated in the faculty handbook. The reasons for which teachers may be absent from school represent a major personnel policy issue.

Sick days, personal days, jury duty

What policy does the school have in regard to sick days and personal days? Can unused leave accumulate? If it can, is there any upward limit of accumulation?

Other necessary absences could result from jury duty or military responsibility, such as the reserves of the armed forces. What compensation will the school give for time off? For example, employers are generally legally obligated to pay the difference between the teacher's regular salary and what he or she is paid by the military or for jury duty.

Maternity leave

The question of maternity leave must also be addressed.

Usually, courts have held that women may continue working throughout their pregnancies, as long as they are able to perform their duties. The U.S. Supreme Court in *Monell v. Dept. of Social Services of the City of New York*, 436 U.S. 658 (1978) affirmed this right of women working in the public sector. The law is less well-developed in the nonpublic sector. However, one could expect that the Supreme Court might require the same protections for women in the private sector.

Sex discrimination and maternity leave

In *Dolter v. Wahlert High School* 483 F. Supp. 266 (1980), a Catholic school was accused of sex discrimination. This interesting case involved an unmarried, pregnant teacher in a Catholic school; the woman's contract was not renewed because of her condition. The plaintiff had informed the principal of her pregnancy, but the teacher was given a contract for the next year. Subsequent to signing the contract, the principal informed the teacher that her contract was being terminated. The teacher brought suit against the school, alleging violation of her rights under Title VII (which prohibits discrimination on the basis of sex). She introduced evidence indicating that

31

male teachers known to have engaged in premarital sex were given contracts.

The school maintained that, if the court held that Title VII provisions applied in the Catholic school, the holding would be a violation of the doctrine of separation of church and state as prescribed by the First Amendment. The school further alleged that the pregnant teacher's condition rendered her unable to meet the qualifications for teaching in a Catholic school, that is, upholding the moral teachings of the Catholic Church. The court stated:

> In deciding plaintiff's claim, the court need not concern itself in *any* way with the content of that code [moral] nor with the substance of Catholic teaching generally. Certainly the court need not pass judgment on the substance of the Catholic Church's moral or doctrinal precepts. The only issues the court need decide are whether these moral precepts, to the extent they constitute essential conditions for continued employment, are applied *equally* to defendant's male and female teachers; and whether Ms. Dolter was in fact discharged *only* because she was pregnant rather than because she had obviously had pre-marital sexual intercourse in violation of defendant's moral code. To decide such strictly sex-based issues would not to any degree entangle this court in defendant's religious mission, doctrines or activities; much less excessively so (p. 270).

The court found that Title VII did govern the Catholic school and that, if the school found the condition of the plaintiff embarrassing, it could have offered her a paid leave of absence instead of terminating her, and thus, inviting a sex discrimination suit.

To date no court has ordered a nonpublic school to reinstate a wrongfully dismissed teacher. Since the remedy for breach of contract is damages, a school found to be in error may well be ordered to pay damages to the wronged party.

The *Dolter* case is similar to the *Bob Jones* case. In *Bob*

Jones the court ruled that the state's compelling interest in racial equality could lead it to deny tax-exempt status to an institution which practiced racial discrimination. In *Dolter* the court refused to allow a Catholic institution to discriminate on the basis of sex. Although the Dolter case is not concerned with the tax-exempt status of the school, one can easily see that persistence in discrimination on the basis of sex might have such an effect.

The dilemma illustrated by these two cases is apparent—any nonpublic school (whether church-related or not) that wants to hold teachers to specific standards of moral conduct to which they might not be held in the public school—should have a written policy clearly delineating the standards. In addition, the school must be fair and consistent in implementing policies. William Valente (1980) comments:

> In the absence of a contrary express contract term, the implication of an obligation not to contradict by public action the religious teachings of the school may apply to a religious school, and it is settled that secular courts will not question the validity of religious precepts of any church (but only their sincerity) since any judicial clauses of the First Amendment (p. 465).

This case illustrates the importance of having clearly written policies with regard to maternity. The *Dolter* court ruled that religious schools do have a right to set standards of conduct, but that those standards must be equally applied to all. Simply because the woman is the one who becomes pregnant and thus shows that she has broken a church law is not a basis for dismissal. The basis for dismissal is the breaking of the church law regarding premarital sex.

A Catholic school could have as policy a statement such as, "All teachers must uphold the teachings of the Catholic Church. Failure to do so may result in dismissal." Such a statement would, of course, encompass many areas. The important factor to keep in mind when developing policies is that, once adopted, they must be applied equally to all.

Paternity leave

More and more fathers are requesting paternity leave. The law is still in a formative stage in this area, but it would seem that the best course of action would be to extend to a father the same benefits that would be given to a mother. For example, a father should be able to use his accumulated sick leave and to take an unpaid leave of absence.

Bereavement leave

Bereavement leave is another potential source of misunderstanding and comparison-making. It is wise, therefore, to state how many days off are allowed and for what degree of kinship. It is generally accepted that a person is allowed time off for the death of a spouse's relative within the same degree of kinship—such as mother, father, sister, brother, grandparents—as would be allowed for one's own relatives. If exceptions can be made, the person responsible for making the exception should be named.

In all leave situations, the principal might wish to add a line stating that the administrator can extend the limits of the leave at his or her discretion. Such a statement allows for the just handling of situations in which the rules simply do not seem to apply. Administrators must be careful to make exceptions only when circumstances warrant them and to avoid the appearance of favoritism.

Grievance procedures

No matter how hard administrators try to be fair and just in their dealings with teachers, honest disagreements can and do arise. Canon law encourages persons to practice subsidiarity, the solving of problems at the lowest possible level. Sometimes agreement cannot be reached between teacher and principal. In extreme cases, grievances may be filed.

If the school or the diocese or the religious congregation does not have a grievance procedure, the pastor or other person with appropriate authority should initiate a plan to develop a grievance procedure. What constitutes matter for a grievance should be clearly defined. All disagreements between teachers and principals are not grievances. The grievance procedure should contain, at minimum, the following sections: (1) definition of terms; (2) purpose of the grievance procedure; (3) the steps in the procedure; (4) delineation of the parties and levels of grievance, including what party or parties have the last word.

Tenure/job protection

A personnel policy of the utmost importance to teachers is that of job protection. Since the 1979 case, *National Labor Relations Board v. Catholic Bishop of Chicago*, 440 U.S. 490 (1979), Catholic schools are not required to allow unionization of employees. If unions were in existence in schools prior to this ruling, they can lawfully remain in place.

Most Catholic schools, particularly grade schools, are not unionized. Tenure, which is not commonplace in the Catholic school system, is generally defined as an expectation of continuing employment, as was discussed in Chapter I. In the public sector, teachers usually attain tenure after three or four years of successful teaching; ordinarily, tenure protects public school teachers against arbitrary dismissals. Although teachers can still be dismissed for cause, due process safeguards must be met.

Although Catholic schools may not have formal tenure systems and, indeed, many contracts across the country are year-to-year contracts, a situation called *de facto* tenure may exist. In fact, many teachers in Catholic schools have an expectation of continuing employment. If a Catholic school dismissed a teacher who had been working in the school for ten years, the court would look at the policies, procedures and past practices of the school system. If teachers are usually retained in the system after three years and rarely, if ever, face non-renewal of contract, *de facto* tenure may be found to exist. While Catholic schools are not bound by constitutional due process, they are bound by common law considerations of fairness.

Termination and/or non-renewal of contract

Most cases involving teachers in both the public and private sectors are concerned with teacher dismissals and/or the non-renewal of contracts. Obviously, a decision to dismiss or not to renew the contract of a teacher is one that an administrator should not make lightly, and it is one that should be made only after other attempts at discipline of the faculty member have been made.

Although the constitutional protections afforded public school teachers are not afforded nonpublic school teachers, both sets of teachers are protected by contract law. Administrators in both schools must honor the provisions of the contract made with the teacher or be able to give legitimate reasons for breaking the contract. Courts will scrutinize both public and private school contracts to insure that the provisions of the contract have been followed. While a private school contract may be far less involved than a public school contract, it is nonetheless a contract. Courts also construe handbooks and policy statements as part of the contract existing between teacher and employer and will hold school officials to the provisions of both documents.

Public school teachers may be discharged for a myriad of reasons. These reasons differ from state to state, sometimes even from school district to school district. For example, the law in the state of Massachusetts prescribes that a teacher shall not be dismissed during the duration of the contract "except for inefficiency, incapacity, conduct unbecoming a teacher or superintendent, insubordination or other good cause" (*General Laws of Education Relating to School Committees as of January 1, 1984* p. 91). The law further specifies the procedural protections which are to be given an employee who is faced with dismissal.

Catholic school administrators should be familiar with the laws governing the dismissal of public school teachers. These laws can serve as guidelines in developing policies and procedures in the Catholic sector.

A quick survey of the laws of any state will reveal the problems involved in defining the causes for dismissal: what is inefficiency? who decides what it is? when is it serious enough to warrant dismissal?

Generally, statutes consider the following as grounds for dismissal:

Incompetency is a term that can encompass any of several conditions: physical or mental incapacity which is permanent and incurable (although federal laws prohibiting discrimination against the handicapped must be observed); lack of knowledge about the subject matter one is contracted to teach or lack of ability to impart that knowledge; failure to adapt to new teaching methods; physical mistreatment of students; violation of school rules; violation of duties; lack of cooperation; negligent conduct; failure to maintain discipline; and personal misconduct in or out of school (L. Przewlocki, personal communication, March 1981).

Insubordination is generally the willful refusal to abide by the rules or the directives of superiors. It can be distinguished from incompetency in that an incompetent person may be involved in the same behavior as an insubordinate person, but the incompetent person is not assumed to be willfully violating duties and rules.

Unprofessional conduct can also encompass a wide range of behaviors. Unprofessional conduct may be the same behavior as personal misconduct. However, while all personal misconduct of teachers can probably be construed as unprofessional conduct, not all unprofessional conduct is personal misconduct. For example, it might be considered unprofessional conduct to discuss school matters at the dinner table if one's school age children are present, even if the children are forbidden to repeat the conversation outside the house. It would be difficult to put that behavior in the same category as personal misconduct, such as sexual offenses or arrest for driving while intoxicated. Delon and Bartman (1979, p. 63) state:

A variety of charges against school employees are

subsumed under the category of "unprofessional conduct". Because standards of professional conduct are not clearly defined, courts tend to require an employer to support such charges with substantial evidence.

Immorality is listed in the statutes of many states as grounds for dismissal. However, it is conceded that different communities have different standards of morality and that those standards change with time. Delon and Bartman (p. 65) observe:

> It is not surprising that persons who lose their positions or certification on this ground [immorality] often urge the courts to declare it unconstitutionally vague. Because of the stigma that attaches to such charges, another frequent allegation is that proper procedural safeguards were not afforded. While sexually related conduct and criminal offenses account for most of the dismissals for immorality, occasionally other forms of misconduct are involved.

Case law indicates that courts differ in their interpretation of what constitutes immorality and what constitutes unfitness to teach. Some courts have held that performing an immoral act may not be justification for terminating employment unless proof is available that the act somehow affects one's ability to teach. (Cf. *Board of Education of Long Beach Unified School District of Los Angeles County v. Jack M.* 566 P. 2d 602, Cal. 1977, which involved a teacher who was dismissed after being arrested for an isolated incident of sexual misconduct. The court ruled that the one incident did not constitute proof of unfitness to teach). Standards of "fitness" are changing. For example, possession of marijuana might not be cause to dismiss a teacher unless the possession of marijuana can be proven to affect teaching performance.

Some states include "catch all" phrases such as "a teacher may be dismissed for any other just cause." Just as administrators are not expected to think of everything which a student could possibly do in the way of misconduct or violation of school rules, state legislatures and school committees are not expected to provide for every occasion that may result in the dismissal of a teacher. For example, if a teacher were found to be innocent of a serious crime such as rape or murder because of insanity, the school board could possibly dismiss him or her even in the absence of a statute covering the specific situation and despite the fact that the teacher had been found innocent. The fact that the teacher had indeed killed or raped someone could render school officials within their rights to dismiss.

Courts will generally apply the "whole record" test in a teacher dismissal case except in situations such as criminal conviction or other gross misconduct. If an administrator is seeking to dismiss a teacher for incompetence, the dismissal will probably not be upheld if it is based on a single incident. The court will consider the whole record of the teacher involved before rendering a decision.

Since public school teachers are bound by contract to observe statutes governing them, a teacher who violates any of the prescribed rules can be legitimately dismissed. At the same time, the administrator and the school committee would have the responsibility of providing reasonable evidence as proof of the validity of their assertions.

Similarly, nonpublic school teachers are bound to the terms of their contract or agreement with the institution that employs them. Teacher violations of contract terms in the nonpublic institution may legitimately result in dismissal.

Catholic school administrators should see that the causes for dismissal and the procedures leading up to dismissal are clearly stated in handbooks. Contracts should include a statement that the faculty member agrees to abide by the regulations in the handbook; many courts consider handbooks to be part of the contract.

Policies should not be contradictory. In 1982, five religious sisters sued the bishop and the superintendent of schools (*Reardon et al. v. LeMoyne, et al.* 454 A. 2d 428 (N.H. 1982) because their contracts were not renewed. Each sister had been in the Catholic school for a length of time that would have resulted in tenure if she had been in the public sector. The major problem was the language of the employment documents. One clause stated that employment ended each year unless definitively renewed. Another clause contained a statement to the effect that a teacher could expect employment until the summer following his or her seventieth birthday. Clearly, the documents were contradictory. Problems could have been avoided if the documents had been checked to be sure that they did not differ. The court ruled that it did have jurisdiction over the civil employment contracts of religious. The parish school board was ordered to give the sisters a hearing, if the sisters desired one. As one can imagine, this is one of those situations in which everybody loses in some way. The sisters lost their jobs; the parish community felt the effects of the conflict; the diocese, no doubt, was affected as well. The Catholic school needs to state its position on contract renewal. Is the contract a year-to-year contract which grants no expectation of continuing employment? Or is it a kind of *de facto* tenure operative in theory or in practice? It is very important that the handbook and the contract be in harmony.

Does a teacher have any recourse in a non-renewal situation? Many schools may wish to provide for some sort of hearing in an effort to be sure that actions are moral as well as legal. If a hearing is to be granted, the persons constituting the hearing board and the process for conducting a hearing must be clearly defined. The person or group that has the "final word" must be identified. In many cases, the bishop is the last court of appeal.

Whatever a given school has as policy, the best assurance that the policy will be followed is having it written into the faculty handbook.

Sample Forms

A final area that should be included in faculty handbooks involves sample forms. These forms will, of course, differ from school to school. It is certainly more practical and efficient to have all forms located in one place. Whatever forms teachers use—report cards, progress reports, deficiencies, detention slips, accident forms, grade change forms—should be included. Such a procedure insures that all teachers know what the "official" forms are and have easy access to them.

Summary

The six areas of philosophy, teaching duties, non-teaching duties, supervision of teachers, personnel policies and sample forms are crucial in the development of a faculty handbook. There are other areas that may be included and which may be important to a given faculty or school.

There is no one right or wrong way to compose a faculty handbook. Each principal has to decide what is important for the faculty. The above is simply a discussion of six areas which ought to be included in some way in every faculty handbook. The points discussed should give principals some "food for thought" as they develop or revise their handbooks.

The six components discussed are broad areas of concern. More experienced administrators may already have legally sound faculty handbooks in place. As new concerns arise, the administrator and other appropriate parties will develop policies and rules to meet the new concerns. Sometimes this kind of reactive approach is unavoidable. Certainly, a proactive approach which attempts to envision possible difficulties is preferable to trying to develop a policy to meet a problem as it arises and seeking to minimize future problems by developing policy after the damage has been done.

A sample faculty handbook outline follows. Since a faculty handbook is generally lengthier than the parent/student handbook and probably includes most of the material in the parent/student handbook as well as faculty policies and procedures, an outline for the faculty handbook is presented. The following two chapters, which will deal with parent/student handbooks and board handbooks, will include checklists but will not include sample outlines.

Administrators may wish to involve teachers, parents and students in developing faculty handbooks. An outline generated by a principal should be more relevant to the school's particular situation.

The outline which follows is based on actual handbooks used in Catholic schools. The questions and comments in each section should enable an administrator to focus on items for inclusion in a faculty handbook. After the statement of philosophy and goals, an alphabetical arrangement of topics is included. This order may prove helpful, especially in the initial organization of the handbook.

Sample Faculty Handbook Outline

Philosophy and goals of the school

In its simplest form a philosophy will answer the question, "What do we, as Catholic educators say that we are doing in this school?" A set of goals will "enflesh" the philosophy, and a set of objectives will suggest strategies for achieving the goals. For example, a philosophy might contain a statement such as, "We believe that the goal of education is the preparation of academically qualified citizens committed to the pursuit of learning and to the service of humankind." One goal might be, "To collaborate with civic and other local communities so that students experience a sharing of education and service with the larger community." A specific objective might be, "To offer experiences of service, both within and outside the school environment."

In Catholic schools one would expect the philosophy to reflect belief in God and commitment to the Catholic faith. The next sections will consider other aspects of school life which follow from philosophy and goals.

Admission of students

What is the school's policy on admission? What qualifications are necessary for a student to be considered for admission? What commitments are expected from students and their parents? The handbook should contain a statement of non-discrimination such as, "The school does not discriminate on the basis of race, sex (in a co-educational school), creed, color, religion or national origin." Financial aid procedures could be included here or under a separate heading.

Although these areas are properly the domain of administration, it is important that faculty be as well informed as possible since teachers are often approached by parents and/or students for this kind of information.

Academics

What subjects are students required to take? In what subjects must students receive a passing grade in order to be promoted or to graduate? How are grades computed? Some direction with regard to standards is in order. What constitutes "A" work or "unsatisfactory" work?

What is the school's or diocese's policy with regard to retention of students? If a student is placed in the next grade because of parental wishes and over the objections of the school's professional staff, how and where is that fact noted? Are parents required to sign a statement that they know the student is being moved to the next grade against professional advice? Is a different term than "promoted" used in such cases? Perhaps students in this situation could be "transferred" rather than "promoted".

What responsibilities does a teacher have towards a student who is experiencing academic difficulties? How does a teacher document fulfillment of these responsibilities?

—

43

Accidents

What should a teacher do if an accident occurs while supervising students? Should an accident form be automatically filed? Should the principal always be notified? Should the student's parents always be notified? (With the increasing amount of litigation taking place, the safest course is to keep some sort of written record regarding any such incident. The author knows of one diocese in which the insurance carrier has directed that the schools document even the dispensing of band-aids to students.)

Activity record(s)

The main office or guidance counselor should keep some record of student involvement in extra-curricular activities, even in the elementary school. What is a teacher's responsibility in this regard? In elementary school, a teacher might keep a card on each student; in junior and senior high school, a homeroom teacher could distribute forms to students and return completed copies to the office.

Announcements

How do teachers receive announcements? Through abulletin board or through written notices placed in mailboxes? How do teachers make announcements that affect the whole school or students other than those they teach?

The answers to these questions can be most important if an incident should occur and a student or teacher should claim that an announcement was never made.

Assignments

Expectations for homework assignments should be stated in this section. How much homework is given to primary, middle, junior, and senior high students? How much time should a teacher expect that students will spend on homework? Should teachers' lesson plan books document assigned homework that is given?

Attendance

What kind of records are homeroom teachers and subject teachers expected to keep? What is the parents' responsibility in reporting absences? What procedure should be followed if a teacher discovers that a student whose name is not on the absentee list is actually missing from class? What is the responsibility of teachers regarding make-up work for absent students?

This section should contain a statement that students may never take attendance. Only teachers and professional staff should check attendance. If a student's absence is not properly recorded and some harm should come to the individual, the school could be held responsible for not noting the absence.

The best legal protection for a school in the reporting of student absence is to follow a policy such as this one: "Parents are to call the school before a given time to report a student's absence. If the parent does not call, the school will call the parent or person designated by the parent as an emergency contact."

Documentation of all such calls and/or attempted calls will be kept.

Classroom teachers

All expectations of classroom teachers not otherwise stated in the handbook should be noted in this section.

Close of school year

What are the professional responsibilities of teachers at the end of a school year? What materials (keys, textbooks, plan books, grade books, *etc.*) can be kept, and what should be left in the school's possession? What, if any, penalties will result from non-compliance?

Department chairpersons/level coordinators

If a school has department chairpersons or level co-ordinators, their duties should be spelled out carefully. Do they approve textbooks? Do they develop curriculum? Do they observe teachers?

Deficiencies and/or progress reports

If the school sends out such student reports, what criteria govern who receives them? What are a teacher's

45

responsibilities in regard to notification of parents and providing remedial assistance if student performance is deficient?

Discipline

The school discipline code should be stated in its entirety. Recommendations for constructive and effective discipline might be included here.

Dress code

If a faculty dress code or dress guidelines exist, these should be included in the faculty handbook.

Extra-curricular activities

The policy concerning faculty members' moderating extra-curricular activities should be stated here, and all responsibilities of moderators should be listed. It is extremely important that moderators understand that they are responsible for the safety of the students and that students cannot be left in the school building or at the site of the school activity without adult supervision.

Faculty meetings

Are all faculty members required to attend faculty meetings? Who is responsible for developing the agenda? How does a teacher place an item on the agenda? Minutes of all meetings should be kept, and each faculty member should receive a copy of the minutes. A copy should be kept on file in the principal's office.

It would be advisable to state that faculty members who are excused from attendance at a faculty meeting are responsible for knowing and implementing any decisions made during that meeting.

Field trips

Must all field trips have an educational purpose, or are strictly recreational trips (such as trips to amusement parks) allowed? Many school law experts believe that all field trips should have some educational purpose. If an accident were to occur, a school could much more easily justify an educational trip than one that is purely recreational.

Who schedules field trips? It would be advisable to have one person keep a master schedule of all field trips.

What permission form is to be used? The following might be a model:

I/We, the parent(s)/guardian(s) of _____ request that the school allow my/our son/daughter to participate in (insert activity/trip).

We hereby release and save harmless the school of _____ and any and all of its employees from any and all liability for any and all harm arising to my/our son/daughter as a result of this trip.

When possible, both parents should sign the form, and any special conditions should be noted. If a trip poses some particular risks, such as being near a lake or walking through a wooded area where poisonous plants might be found, these should be noted.

If there is not a standard mode of transportation (such as school buses), the type of transportation for this trip should be noted, and parents should sign that they accept the mode which is being used. If parents are driving private cars, they should be told whether the school has insurance covering the use of private cars. If the school does not have insurance, parents should be notified of that fact and should understand that they can be held personally liable in the event of accident or injury. Parent volunteer drivers could be asked to furnish proof of possession of insurance. The same cautions apply when teachers use their own cars. Thus, the use of teacher cars should be discouraged.

The ratio of children to adult chaperones should be stated. Generally, the rule is that the younger the children are chronologically or mentally, the greater the standard of care. A good ratio might be one adult to every ten students. With very small children, one adult for every seven or eight children might be considered.

Procedures for checking forms for forgery should be

47

in place; spot checks are one way. The teacher responsible for the field trip could be required to check signatures with those that are on file in the office. Perhaps the school secretary could be given the task of checking all field trip forms. When one person consistently checks all forms, the likelihood of finding forgeries increases.

A student who does not have a signed permission form should not be allowed to go the trip. A phone call from a parent should not be accepted in place of the signed form.

Fire drills

Procedures for fire drills must be clearly stated, and responsibilities of teachers must be defined.

If there is a procedure to settle faculty grievances, it should be included here. This procedure may be one developed by the diocese or the local school board.

Guidance department

If the school has a guidance department, its functions should be stated. Procedures for student referral should be included.

Sickness/leaves of absence

What should a faculty member do regarding professional duties when ill? Who should be notified? If the principal cannot be reached, is there someone else who can be called? Should lesson plans be made available? Are teachers expected to keep a file of student activities (games, *etc.*) that can be used in a teacher's absence?

Sick leave

A sick leave policy should answer the following questions:
1. How many days per year may be taken as sick leave?
2. For what reasons may sick leave be taken, i.e., spouse or child illness?
3. Does sick leave accumulate?

4. Will a teacher be paid for sick day(s) taken before or after a holiday?
5. May an administrator require a doctor's certificate?

Temporary leaves of absence—personal days

The same questions as asked regarding sick leave would apply here. Leaves of absence for personal business, bereavement, armed forces' reserve duty, and jury duty should be discussed. Are there any constraints concerning when these days may be taken?

Maternity/paternity leave

Is maternity leave paid or unpaid? How long is it? Is paternity leave allowed? When should a teacher notify the administrator of intent to take leave?

Illness (student)

What procedures should a teacher follow if a student arrives ill, becomes ill in class or during some other school activity? Where should such students be sent? Should another student accompany the ill student?

Leaving the school grounds

May a teacher leave the grounds during the school day? If a teacher should leave, what procedures should be followed?

Non-teaching duties

Responsibilities of teachers for non-teaching duties not otherwise discussed in the handbook could be listed here. Some examples might be: study hall presiding, cafeteria and playground monitoring, attendance at meetings, religious exercises, *etc.*

Phone/parent conferences

What are the school's expectations regarding conferences with parents in person or by phone? Is a teacher expected to return a parent's phone call within a certain number of hours? What record will the school keep of parent phone calls to teachers? What records of conversations with parents should teachers keep?

Policies of the school

Some schools have a separate section for policies not mentioned elsewhere. For example, policies regarding pregnant students might be included here. Expectations regarding teacher participation/presence during assemblies and other activities could also be stated in this section.

Principal/vice-principal

In a parish school, the pastor generally appoints the principal after consultation with the school board. Principals of diocesan schools may be appointed by the superintendent. Religious congregations or school boards may appoint the principal of a school owned by a religious congregation. The process and power of appointment should be clearly defined.

How is a vice-principal appointed? What is the term of office? If the principal leaves office, does the new principal have the right to appoint a new vice-principal? Will the vice-principal be offered a full teaching position? The job descriptions and responsibilities of the school's chief administrators should be stated.

Supervision and evaluation of teachers

Who supervises teachers? How often can a teacher expect to be visited? What supervisory format will be followed? Will there be pre and post conferences? Will the supervisory instrument become a part of the teacher's file? Are unscheduled classroom visits permitted and/or encouraged? How are teachers evaluated? Do teachers have the right to append their own opinions to supervisory reports and evaluations that become part of personnel files?

Termination of teachers/summary dismissal

If these topics are not discussed elsewhere, they should be included here. What are the procedures for teacher dismissal/non-renewal of contract? Does a teacher have any recourse and, if so, what is it?

The above outline is simply a suggestion of topics that could be included. An administrator might wish now to consider topics that could be pertinent to a particular school or other topics relevant to a handbook. The important action for an administrator to take is a commitment to developing or revising a faculty handbook according to the needs and philosophy of the school and according to sound legal principles.

PARENT/STUDENT HANDBOOKS

A Catholic school, like all other schools, needs to insure that both parents and students understand the rules and policies of the school and agree to be governed by those rules and policies. Some Catholic schools have separate handbooks for parents and students. This author believes that having one handbook for both parents and students is preferable to having separate handbooks. The school should ask the parents to discuss the handbook with their children. In this way, families are able to participate as a unit in the life of the school. Parents share the responsibility for their children's understanding the philosophy of the school and the rules that flow from that philosophy. Parents and students should be asked to sign a statement that they have read and discussed the handbook and that they agree to support its provisions.

If a school decides to have separate handbooks for parents and students, parents should be asked to sign a statement that they have read and agree to accept the provisions of both handbooks.

When administrators consider handbooks, rules and regulations come to mind. Most school officials and lawyers would agree that the best school law is, like medicine, preventive. The best defense is having tried to follow the right course in the first place. School officials must realize that, despite their best efforts in any and all areas of school life (student discipline, faculty discipline, safety, *etc.*), they may well face lawsuits. All schools must look carefully at their rules and procedures to be confident that they are reasonable, fair and consistent—or else be prepared to risk lawsuits.

E. Edmund Reutter, Jr. (1975), after analyzing hundreds of school cases, offers six minimum essentials for developing enforceable rules of conduct. These essentials are: (1) the rule must be published to students; (2) the rule must have a legitimate educational purpose; (3) the rule must have a rational relationship to the achievement of the stated educational purpose; (4) the meaning of the rule must be reasonably clear; (5) the rule must be sufficiently narrow in scope so as not to encompass constitutionally-protected activities along with those which may be constitutionally prohibited in the school setting; and (6) if the rule infringes upon a fundamental constitutional right of students, a compelling interest of the school (which is a government agent) in the enforcement of the rule must be shown (pp. 68-69). While the fifth and sixth rules do not apply to nonpublic schools, all the rules are worth considering when drawing up a school disciplinary code.

As stated in Chapter I, Catholic schools are not bound by the same constitutional constraints that oblige public schools because Catholic schools are not arms of the state. The prevailing law in the Catholic school is contract law. Nonetheless, Catholic school administrators would be well advised to know what freedoms are protected in the public sector and to be prepared to offer some reasonable rationale for rules adopted that are not protective of those freedoms. Catholic schools may have dress codes that would not be permitted in a public school. Catholic schools may demand that students and teachers participate in religious exercises and refrain from speech that is critical of the Catholic Church.

Assuming that the rules of a school have been properly

developed, promulgated and implemented, one must then determine the appropriate procedures to be followed when rules are violated, particularly when the infractions are repeated.

Courts assume that school officials are impartial parties and will give students fair hearings. Decisions in both public and nonpublic school cases insist that fairness is part of the responsibility incumbent upon school personnel as part of the school's contract with students and parents.

Courts look for evidence of good faith: did the institution have a rule that was promulgated? did the student know of the rule? The court does not concern itself with the wisdom of the rule—or even with the rightness or wrongness of the professional opinion of educators. The court is only concerned with the existence of a properly promulgated rule and with the institution's acting in good faith according to the procedures it stated would be followed.

Courts look to the Constitution for guidance in determining whether public school students' rights have been violated. In all school cases (whether public or nonpublic), courts look for basic fairness in the execution of the contract existing between the student/ parent and the school when the student is alleging that a school acted improperly in its imposition of disciplinary sanctions.

School officials must understand that they will never be able to write down everything a student might possibly do that can result in disciplinary sanctions. Therefore, it is advisable to have some kind of "catch-all" clause such as "other inappropriate conduct." No court will expect a school to have written down all possible offenses, but courts will expect that *something* is written down and that students and parents have a reasonable idea of the expectations of the school.

Catholic educators must be concerned with being models of mature, responsible, Christian behavior. Disciplinary policies and procedures must be examined in the light of responsible behavior.

As in the construction of the faculty handbook, the beginning point for rules' development should be the school's philosophy. Every school should have a clearly-written philosophy that is available to all members of the school community. Even first graders can be brought to some understanding of philosophy: "At our school we try to treat each other in the way Jesus would want us to act." The life of the school should be seen as flowing from the philosophy.

Rules are just one more facet of school life and should carry out the philosophy. For example, it would seem inconsistent with a philosophy promoting the development of mature, educated citizens to state, "Students are never allowed excused absences from school without a doctor's note." Such a rule, besides being unreasonable in terms of illness, would preclude provisions for other necessary absences, such as attendance at funerals, etc.

Rules should be clear and understandable. The test that might be applied by the courts could be the following: would two persons of average intelligence reading this rule have the same understanding of it? A rule stating, "Students arriving at class after the bell has rung will be marked tardy" is clear while a rule such as "Late students will be marked tardy" is open to such questions as: how late is late? after the bell? after the teacher begins class?

Whenever possible, rules should be written as there are certainly common sense reasons for writing rules. When emotions run high, it is easier to pick up the written rule than to insist that "at the beginning of school you were told thus and such."

Having a written handbook should encourage the school to strive for clarity in rule-making. Periodic evaluation would enable the school to make necessary changes.

The checklist in Exhibit 2 (page 57) may help the administrator judge what is needed in any parent/student handbook and what specific additions, deletions and/or revisions would strengthen the handbook currently in use.

EXHIBIT 2 CHECKLIST FOR PARENT/STUDENT HANDBOOKS		
	What should a school have concerning?	**What does my school need?**
Philosophy/Goals		
Admission Policies (non-discriminatory)		
Academic Policies		
Communication Parent/Teacher Teacher/Parent Administration		
Discipline Code		
Extra-curricular Activities		
Field Trip Policies/Forms		
Parent Service Requirements		
Parent(s)'/Student's Signed Agreement		
Principal's Right to Amend		
Use of School Grounds		

School Philosophy

As stated throughout this work, the school philosophy is basic and should be included in all handbooks. Every member of the school community and, indeed, all who come into contact with a school, should see that persons are striving to live out the philosophy which governs the school.

If the staff of a school believes that the philosophy is written in language that is beyond the understanding of the students, an abridged or otherwise paraphrased philosophy might be prepared. What school officials should seek is a situation in which every member of the community could offer a simple explanation of the philosophy when asked: "Here we try to live as Jesus would want us to live and to learn our lessons as best we can."

Admission Policies

Non-discriminatory statement

As the *Bob Jones* and *Dolter* cases indicate, nonpublic schools are required to treat all people equally. In the Catholic school, there can be no discrimination on the basis of race, sex (unless traditionally a single sex school), national origin, age (in accordance with the law), and handicapping condition (if, with reasonable accommodation on the part of the school, the handicapped person could be accommodated).

Preference for Catholic students

Catholic schools may discriminate on the basis of religion. Meaning that Catholic schools may give preference to Catholic students. However, if there is an admissions' preference, it should be stated in writing. For example, a school might say: "This school gives preference in admission to Catholic students living within the parish boundaries; secondly, to Catholic students living outside the parish boundaries; thirdly, to non-Catholics."

Financial Policies

Financial obligations should be clearly stated and tuition for a given year should be indicated. Refund policies for entrance fees, tuition, book purchases should also be noted. Much ill will can be avoided if parents are told from the very beginning what monies will be refunded.

Academic Policies

Homework

The school's or the diocese's policy with regard to homework should be stated here, as it is in the faculty handbook. Parents should be informed as to how much time a student at any given grade level ought to spend on homework. The role that the school expects the parents to take in helping with homework should also be clarified.

Grading

The grading policies of the school should be explained. Whatever system is used (numerical, letter or any other type of grade) should be defined. Statements as to what constitutes superior, satisfactory, and unsatisfactory work should be given.

Absence

Courts have handed down differing opinions as to whether academic penalties can be imposed for absence in the public school; no case has been heard by the Supreme Court to date. Thus, there are no clear guidelines for Catholic schools.

In general, it would be advisable to follow whatever the diocese sets as a guideline and to state the rules in the handbook. Parents should be required to telephone the school if a child is going to be absent. When a child is absent and the parents have not called, the school should telephone the parents. This procedure is the best way to insure that parents know whether their children are in or out of school. In the unfortunate and often dangerous situation in which a child has been sent to school but never arrives, many valuable hours can be lost if the school does not contact the parent about the child's absence.

Promotion/retention

Promotion and retention policies should be discussed. Many dioceses have clear guidelines concerning reasons for which a student may be retained in a grade. If the diocese or school permits a student's entering the next grade simply because a parent wishes the student to be in the next grade, the documentation that will be kept should be noted. In any case, when a student is transferred over the advice of the professional staff, parents should be required to sign a statement that they realize that the transfer is against the professional advice of the staff. Such documentation can protect the school if, at a later date, allegations are made that the student should not have been placed in the next grade. In such a case it may be legally advisable to refer to the child's movement to the next grade as a transfer and not as a promotion.

Records

Prior to 1975, parents and students did not have any rights with regard to viewing their records. In 1975, the Buckley Amendment, also known as the Family Educational Rights and Privacy Act, gave parents and students the right of access to records and the right to request that statements be changed or deleted. If the school refuses to change or delete records, statements made by parents or students should be included in the record.

Although no Supreme Court case involving Catholic schools and rights of access to records has been brought by parents or students, Catholic schools would be well advised to follow the regulations in the Buckley Amendment.

The school should state what procedures are to be followed if a parent or student wishes to view a record. The school can ask for twenty-four hours' notice and can require the parent to make the request in writing.

One way that any school can safeguard itself against legal problems in the area of records is to limit what is kept in the official file. The following should be placed in a student's official folder: academic transcripts; academic testing; health records (unless kept in a health office); and an emergency sheet. Any other records (particularly disciplinary ones) can and should be kept elsewhere. School officials must understand that only the contents of the official file should be forwarded to a new school.

Non-custodial parent

The rights of non-custodial parents should be included here. The law holds that parents do not cease to be parents when they no longer have custody of their children. Therefore, schools may wish to include a statement such as:

> This school abides by the provisions of the Buckley Amendment with respect to the rights of non-custodial parents. In the absence of a court order to the contrary, a school will provide the non-custodial parent with access to the academic records and to other school-related information regarding the child. If there is a court order specifying that there is to be no information given, it is the responsibility of the custodial parent to provide the school with an official copy of the court order.

Another way to handle the non-custodial parent situation is to ask all divorced parents to furnish the school with a copy of the custody section of the divorce decree. This information will also help the school in determining when, if ever, the child can be released to the non-custodial parent.

Communication

Many problems can be avoided if the school handbook states the procedures by which parents contact school officials, and school officials contact parents.

In keeping with the church's principle of subsidiarity, problems should be solved at the lowest level whenever possible. Thus, it would seem advisable that persons having a problem with another individual go directly to that person before going to that person's superior. If a parent has a complaint about a teacher, it seems only just that the parent discuss the difficulty first with the teacher.

If a parent is reluctant to confront a teacher alone, the administrator might offer to be present at a conference. Requiring persons to attempt to work out their difficulties mutually is certainly consistent with the demands of the Gospel and makes good legal sense as well.

If a parent wishes to communicate with a teacher, how should contact be made? Spontaneous visits to a classroom ought to be discouraged, but a parent could be directed to make an appointment by telephone or letter. If the teacher wishes to contact the parent, how might the parent expect that this contact will be made? Parents need such information.

How should a parent contact an administrator? If an appointment is necessary, how should it be made? Obviously, there are times when informal contacts will occur. There are also times when everyone will profit if people have an opportunity to distance themselves from the situation before discussing it. Thus, the existence of a procedure for communication can be helpful.

Discipline Code

Rules/penalties/exceptions

As this work has indicated, the school should strive for simplicity and clarity in rule construction; long lists of rules should probably be avoided. Phrases such as "other inappropriate behavior" or "conduct unbecoming a Christian student" cover many types of misbehavior. Examples of infractions could be provided.

The principal or other administrator should retain the right to make exceptions. There may be a case in which mitigating circumstances call for a different response than has been the norm in the past. A phrase such as, "the principal is the final recourse in all disciplinary situations and may waive any disciplinary rule for just cause at his or her discretion" may be in order. It is true that this may appear to be inviting everyone to seek to be an exception; however, this author believes it is better to take that risk than to "box" one's self into a corner with rules that offer no flexibility.

Phrases such as "must" or "will result in a certain penalty" can result in little or no leeway. Phrases such as "can" or "may" give a disciplinarian room to allow for individual circumstances.

Generally, diocesan handbooks will offer guidance in the area of student discipline and rules'development and promulgation.

Due process/appeals

While considering the development of procedural due process guidelines, educators should be aware that there is a time investment involved. If a teacher allows a student to tell his or her story instead of summarily imposing punishment ("All students whose names are on the board will remain after school"), the teacher makes a commitment to spending time with a student who faces discipline. The principal or disciplinarian makes a commitment to listening to the student's side of the the story as well as to the teacher's, and the benefit should be obvious: students perceive teachers and administrators as trying to be fair and, one hopes, will internalize the values thus modeled.

All Catholic schools, then, should commit themselves, to notice and a hearing in any disciplinary situation; in this way, the school is meeting the minimum requirements of due process. This commitment would mean that the student is told what he or she did that was wrong and is given a chance to be heard.

Somewhat more extensive procedures should be developed if the penalty is suspension. One-day suspensions, at minimum, should require that the principal be involved and that the parents be notified. Longer suspensions should involve the same notification but should also include a written notice of the charges and an indication of the time and place of the hearing. Cases in which the possibility of expulsion exists require a more formal notification and hearing at which the student should be able to confront accusers. Careful documentation must be kept in all major disciplinary proceedings.

Public schools may be required to grant a student facing expulsion the right to bring legal counsel to the hearing. Catholic schools, however, should avoid the presence of legal counsel. To allow a student to bring an attorney could be setting a precedent. The presence of attorneys often results in an adversarial situation which can make the achievement of any sort of pastoral reconciliation very difficult.

This discussion of discipline should be helpful to Catholic school principals and faculties as they attempt to develop and modify rules and policies. The guiding principle in any discussion of discipline and due process should be the desire to act in a Christian manner characterized by fairness and compassion.

Maternity/paternity policies

Catholic schools, elementary as well as secondary, are faced with the situations of unwed mothers and fathers. This issue is certainly an emotionally charged one. School officials need to consider carefully the consequences of any policies that are adopted. At the very minimum, students should be allowed to finish their work and receive grades and diplomas.

Although some parents and teachers may believe that pregnant students do not belong in school, school officials should ponder what kind of messages students receive if unwed parents are excluded from school. Is a real, if unintended, message being sent that abortion is an answer that will help the student to save face and continue in the Catholic school? Is a situation such as the *Dolter* case being constructed in which the young woman is discriminated against because she is the one who becomes pregnant while the young man can deny his involvement?

Whether the unwed parent is allowed to participate in such activities as commencement is a difficult question. At the very least a school should consider a statement such as, "Pregnancy is not a reason for dismissal from school." To do otherwise seems to indicate an unwillingness to support a student who has made a choice to give life, rather than to end it.

Extra-curricular Activities

All extra-curricular activities sponsored by the Catholic school should be listed, along with the requirements for participation. If certain academic and conduct standards must be maintained for participation, these should be noted.

Any other policies that may be in effect should also be stated. If, for example, a student must be in school in order to participate in a sport or other activity on a given day, that fact should be clarified.

As far as possible, the same standards for all extra-curricular activities should be set and maintained. It does not seem fair for a football player to be denied participation because of low grades, if a drama club member with similar academic standing can continue in the club simply because state or diocesan standards govern only participation in athletics.

Field Trip Policies/Forms

Privilege not a right

Field trips are privileges afforded to students; no student has an absolute right to a field trip. The school handbook should state that field trips are privileges and that students can be denied participation if they fail to meet academic or behavioral requirements.

Standard permission form

It is an excellent practice to include a copy of the school's permission form in the handbook. Then, if a student forgets to bring the form home, a parent can copy the proper form from the book and fill in the appropriate date and place. Schools should not accept forms other than the one the school had adopted.

Letters stating, "John can go with you today," simply provide no legal protection for the school.

The handbook should state that students who fail to submit a proper form will not be allowed to participate in the field trip. The handbook should also state that telephone calls will not be accepted in lieu of proper forms.

The right of parents to refuse to allow their child to participate in a field trip might also be mentioned.

Liability of school

Although no parent can sign away a child's right to safety, a handbook should state that the parents are expected to sign the permission form which releases the school from liability. School officials must understand, of course, that there is no such protection from the consequences of negligent behavior on the part of school staff; however, a proper form offers a school as much protection as can be had.

Parent Service Requirement

Many Catholic schools today find that they cannot operate without support beyond that provided by tuition. It is perfectly legitimate to require parents to give some sort of service in addition to the payment of tuition. However, parents must be told of this requirement when enrolling their children.

The handbook should define what is expected. Is the parent required to give a certain number of hours of service to the school? What sorts of activities meet these requirements? Is the parent or student expected to participate in fund-raising? Is there any alternative? (For example, can a parent pay an additional fee and thus avoid service?) What is the penalty for non-participation?

Parent organizations

The names and functions of all school or school-related organizations to which parents may belong should be listed, along with requirements for participation.

The role of the school board, if there is one, should be defined and the method for making contact with the board should be stated.

Use of School Grounds

Case law indicates that schools can be held responsible for accidents on playgrounds or school property before or after school. Some schools have a policy stating that children are not to arrive before a specified time and are to leave by a certain hour. But it is a policy or rule that is often not enforced. No school official wants to be insensitive to the problems of working parents; however, it is not fair for parents to assume that it is permissible to drop children at school very early in the morning and/or to pick them up very late in the afternoon. It is also not fair to assume that teachers or principals who arrive at school early or who stay late will be responsible for children. If a child is injured while on school property during an unsupervised time, a court will look to the parent/student handbook to see if a policy is in place, and if it has been enforced.

Athletic practices and other activities, such as parish-sponsored programs, pose problems as well. The question of supervision must be addressed in the handbook, and parents must know what the school will and will not do.

There are several approaches to this supervision problem. One is to post "no trespassing" signs and enforce a policy of no student presence on school grounds outside specified times. If a student is on the grounds at a time when no supervision is provided, the parents should be notified. Appropriate warnings and penalties should be given. The school and the school board might want to consider a policy that would require parents to withdraw a child from school after repeated offenses.

Another approach would be to provide funds to pay someone to supervise before and after school. With more and more schools adding day care and after school care programs, another solution is possible. A policy could be developed stating that any child who is present in the school building or on the ground at proscribed times will be placed in day care and the parents will be billed for the service.

There are, of course, other options; the important thing is to do something. Do not take refuge in the belief that since nothing has ever happened, nothing will. One lawsuit could be extremely costly and could perhaps be avoided if rules, policies and procedures had been developed and enforced.

School/Principal's Right to Amend Handbook

It is advisable to add a clause stating that the school or the principal retains the right to amend the handbook for just cause and that parents will be given prompt notification if changes are made.

Agreements Signed by Parents and Students

For everyone's protection, parents and students should be asked to sign a statement such as, "We have read and agree to be governed by this handbook." Such a statement avoids many of the problems that can arise when parents or students state that they did not know such a rule existed.

A school would be well advised not to admit a student to classes until such a signed agreement is submitted. Since courts construe handbooks as part of the contract existing between the school and the parents/students, it is both legally and ethically wise to insure that all parties to the contract have read it and agree to be ruled by it.

SCHOOL BOARD HANDBOOKS

C atholic school boards are somewhat recent phe-
nomena in the history of Catholic education. The
years since Vatican II have witnessed the laity's taking an increasing role in the governance of Catholic
schools. School board membership is one way that the
laity share in the teaching ministry of the church. Certainly, at no time in our history has the role of the school
board been more important than it is now.

School administrators should find boards to be a
source of support and strength. The relationships between and among pastors, principals and board members
should be mutually beneficial. In order for the maximum
good to be achieved by board members, pastors and
principals working together, it is important that the role
of the board be carefully delineated and the scope of its
authority defined. Board members have a right to expect
that they will be given the information and documents
which they need in order to perform their job effectively.

Board members must understand that their only real
power is vested in the board acting as a board. Individual board members have no actual power and should
guard against receiving complaints from parents and
teachers that should be brought to appropriate school
officials instead of to board members.

Principals are often called upon to provide board members with pertinent information. In some cases, principals are expected to compile a handbook for board members. Since a board handbook will include documents already discussed at length in this work, faculty handbooks and parent/student handbooks, this chapter will briefly discuss other elements that should be present in a board handbook. Persons desiring more in-depth information concerning legal ramifications of school board membership are directed to the 1988 NCEA publication, *A Primer on School Law: A Guide for Board Members in*

EXHIBIT 3 BOARD HANDBOOK CHECKLIST		
	What should a school board have concerning?	**What do we need?**
Philosophy		
By-laws/Constitutions		
Policies: Actual or Sample 　　Principal 　　Personnel 　　Students/Parents 　　Plant 　　Finances		
Formal Minutes		
Financial Information 　　Budgets 　　Audits 　　Other		
Confidentiality		

Catholic Schools.

Canon, or church law, governs Catholic schools. Catholic schools and board members have no authority to act outside the provisions of canon law. Within the provisions of canon law, however, Catholic schools have great freedom so long as no civil laws are broken. Catholic school boards have much wider latitude in the development of policies and rules than do their public school counterparts.

The checklist in Exhibit 3 may be helpful to school administrators in developing or revising a board handbook or manual.

Philosophy

It is crucial that board members understand and "own" the philosophy of the school. Board members probably have less day- to-day contact with the lived experience of the school than do faculty, students, administrators, and some parents. Thus, it is essential that board members be thoroughly familiar with the philosophy and be able to base actions and decisions upon it.

By-laws/Constitutions

Written by persons with authority

Every school board should have by-laws and/or constitutions. Some dioceses provide parishes with such documents and each board is expected to follow the same general format.

In the case of private schools or schools owned by religious congregations, the appropriate supervisory party should supply the necessary documents.

Adopted/accepted by the board

According to the by-laws and/or constitutions, the board members should adopt or accept the governance document. Board members should be given a thorough orientation to the philosophy and the governance document before beginning membership on the board or as soon as possible thereafter.

Appropriate Components

1. Scope of authority. There are four types of schools in our Catholic system: parish, inter-parish, diocesan and schools owned by religious communities. The 1987 NCEA publication, *A Primer on Educational Governance in the Catholic Church,* adopts two main models for boards of Catholic schools that are owned by the diocese: consultative (often called advisory in the past) and boards with limited jurisdiction (often called policy-making).

A consultative board is one generally established by the pastor or by diocesan policy. This board has responsibilities for the development and/or approval of policies. The pastor has the final authority to accept the recommendations of the consultative board. Even though a consultative board is, strictly speaking, advisory, the school's best interests would be served if the board is able to use a consensus model of decision-making whenever possible. Consensus does not necessarily mean that everyone agrees that a certain action is the best possible or one's own personal preference; rather, consensus means that all members have agreed to support the decision for the sake of the school.

A board with limited jurisdiction has been defined as one "constituted by the pastor to govern the parish education program, subject to certain decisions which are reserved to the pastor and the bishop" (CACE/NABE 27). This type of board would have, in both theory and practice, more autonomy in decision-making than would the consultative board because the pastor has delegated decision-making power to the board with limited jurisdiction. Pastors and bishops can delegate power, but they cannot delegate their ultimate responsibility for actions taken in their parish or diocese.

Private schools owned by religious congregations o

other bodies, such as boards of trustees, may have either consultative boards or boards with limited jurisdiction. The board of a school owned by a religious congregation would relate to the administrator of the religious congregation in the same way a parish school board relates to a pastor. Private schools may also utilize a type of structure called a "corporate board," by which those operating the school would incorporate under state law. This corporate body would be the ultimate authority except in those areas reserved to the bishop (CACE/NABE, p. 36).

2. **Role of the board.** The school board has specific responsibilities to the diocese and to the parish or sponsoring congregation. The school board must insure that its policies are consistent with those of the diocese or sponsoring party. Even private Catholic schools not owned by the diocese are subject to the bishop in matters of faith and morals and may not call themselves "Catholic schools" without his approval.

As this work has cited, cases involving faith and morals can be very complex. Diocesan policy may state that only Catholics who actively practice their religion in accordance with the teachings of the Church may be hired in schools owned and operated by the diocese or parishes within the diocese. But who defines what is a practicing Catholic? The situation of the divorced Catholic contracting a second marriage without an annulment of the first marriage is perhaps the one most often faced by Catholic schools. Even if the person in question is convinced that he or she is acting in good conscience in contracting a marriage outside the Church, there is little doubt that the person is, objectively speaking, a probable source of scandal. This situation is not a problem from the standpoint of terminating the employment of a person who violates Church law, but there are cases in which teachers have sued Catholic schools after being dismissed for contracting such marriages. The courts have always supported the school's right to hold its employees to its teachings and to dismiss those who act at variance with them. The problem is the lack of consistency from diocese to diocese, from school to school, and even within the same school.

A board will not make the decision to terminate a teacher's employment, but since the board suggests and/or approves policy, it must support a decision that is based on diocesan and/or school policy. The board's role is to review any case brought to it on appeal to see that basic fairness has been met and that the school or principal has followed the appropriate policies; its role is not to state whether it would have made the same decision.

A word of caution is in order. The policies and procedures governing termination and/or non-renewal of contract must be clearly written and understood by all those affected. If staff members can be eliminated because of the need to reduce employees, this policy should be stated as should the process by which it is implemented. If appointment to certain positions is dependent upon board or principal approval, that fact should also be stated.

School boards have responsibilities to the principal. Today many school boards appoint the principal or recommend appointment to the pastor or other appropriate person. The board's first duty is to insure that the person selected meets the qualifications set by the diocese or sponsoring congregation.

Since the principal is responsible to the school board as well as to others, the principal should report to the board the method used to insure that board policies are implemented. In order to meet its obligations to parents, students, teachers and staff, the board should annually review handbooks to be sure they are consistent with policy and should accept them as a matter of record. Such review and acceptance strengthens the authority of the principal and insures that the rights and responsibilities of all members of the school community are respected.

3. Membership . By-laws, constitutions, or resolutions should state minimum and maximum numbers of board members. In the case of a school owned by a religious community, there may be a requirement that a certain percentage of the board be members of the religious community. Any such requirements should be clearly defined.

It is most important that length of terms be a matter of policy. Boards that do not state a maximum number of years of membership can find that there is little or no "new blood," and the structure can become somewhat inflexible. The best model might be one that would call for two terms of two or three years each, after which a member would have to "retire" for at least a year.

The method of nominating and electing members should be determined and made available to all interested persons. The titles and responsibilities of board officers should be a matter of policy, as well as the process for electing officers. Standing committees should be named and their functions described.

Any annual or other meeting requirements should be clearly a matter of record.

Policies

Whether a board is consultative or one with limited jurisdiction, its function must be understood in terms of policy, a term generally defined as a guide for action. Policy will dictate what the board wishes to be done, but policy is not concerned with administration or implementation. Thus, the board should not become involved with how its directives will be implemented or with the specific persons who will implement them. For example, a board might state as policy that students are to wear uniforms. The board would not be concerned with which company provides the uniforms or with what color they are. Such questions are administrative ones and they are to be dealt with by the principal who is the chief administrator of the school. Administrative decisions are the day-to-day management choices of the principal. It is important for everyone to understand these distinctions from the beginning.

Generally, boards will set policies in these major areas: administration, personnel, students/parents, plant, and finances.

The board is responsible to insure that the administration is implementing policies. The board probably also has some responsibility in evaluating the principal's job performance, at least in relationship to the board. Recently, many experts are suggesting that evaluation of the principal can best be done by other educational experts with the board giving appropriate input. In any case, the board should insure that evaluation of the principal is being conducted according to policy.

Personnel policies concerning hiring and dismissal procedures, as well as grievance procedures, are the province of the board. It is important to note that the board should not be concerned with who is hired and who is dismissed, but rather that hiring and terminating are conducted according to policy. If the board functions at any level as part of an appeals process, the board should understand that it is to determine whether policies and procedures were fairly followed, not whether it agrees with the final decision.

A board meets its obligations to students and parents by approving program goals, handbooks and other policies.

If a parish council or other body does not have the responsibility for the school plant, the school board may have that duty. The board must insure that building safety is a priority and that all civil codes are met.

The board also will have either advisory or policy-making input regarding tuition setting, salary scales and budget approval.

Formal Minutes

Formal minutes of all board meetings should be kept. Board members should be responsible for filing these minutes in their handbooks and keeping them in good order so they can be passed on to their successors.

Financial Information

Whatever financial information is needed by board members should be made available to them. Depending on the board's degree of responsibility for finances, budgets and audits should be made available, as appropriate.

Confidentiality

Board members have a sacred responsibility to keep the confidences they receive in their capacities as board members. This responsibility should be stressed in orientation and from time to time to be sure that no board member loses sight of this trust.

.

TORT LIABILITY: SOME SPECIAL CONSIDERATIONS

C ivil lawsuits brought by teachers, parents and/ or students against schools and administrators are usually in the nature of tort suits. A tort is a wrong "other than breach of contract" (Black, p. 1335); therefore, the law governing tort cases in the private sector will not be law but will be the same law which is applied to the public school, tort law.

Although the public school district may enjoy some governmental immunity from prosecution (and to a lesser extent, so do its employees), no such immunity exists for the private school and its administrators or other employees. While basically the same kinds of tort suits will arise in the private as well as the public sector (with the exception of constitutional torts), the Catholic school administrator may have fewer defenses than are available to public school counterparts.

Tort suits generally can be classified according to four categories in schools: (1) negligence; (2) corporal punishment; (3) search and seizure; and (4) defamation. Students will most often bring suit under the first three categories, though employees and any others who have been injured at the school may also bring negligence suits. Defamation suits may be brought by students who seek to show wrongful expulsion or other disciplinary measures. It seems more likely, however, that teachers who are disciplined by school officials or whose contracts are terminated or not renewed will bring defamation suits.

Negligence

Negligence is the most common of all lawsuits filed against teachers and administrators (Gatti and Gatti, 1983). Even though negligence is the "fault" against which administrators must guard most constantly, it is also the most difficult type of case about which to predict an accurate judicial outcome. What may be considered negligence in one court may not be so considered in another. It is much better, obviously, to avoid being accused of negligence in the first place than to take one's chances on the outcome of a lawsuit. Gatti and Gatti (1983) have defined negligence as "the unintentional doing or not doing of something which wrongfully causes injury to another" (p. 246). There are four elements which must be present before negligence can exist. These elements, which have been defined by many legal writers, are: duty, violation of a duty, proximate cause and injury. If any one of the four elements is missing, no negligence, and hence, no tort can be found to exist. Since negligence is the unintentional act which results in an injury, a person charged with negligence is generally not going to face criminal charges or spend time in prison.

An examination of each of the four elements necessary to constitute a finding of negligence should be helpful. First, the person charged with negligence must have had a duty in the situation. Students have a right to safety, and teachers and administrators have a responsibility to protect the safety of all entrusted to their care. Teachers are assumed to have a duty to provide reasonable supervision of their students. It is expected that administrators have developed rules and regulations which guide teachers in providing for student safety. Teachers will generally not be held responsible for injuries occurring at a place where, or at a time when, they had no responsibility. A student injured on the way to school normally will not be able to demonstrate that a teacher or administrator had a duty to protect that individual.

However, administrators should be aware of the fact that courts may hold them responsible for student behavior and its consequences occurring on school property before or after school.

William Valente (1980, p. 358) comments: "Beyond the duty to supervise school grounds during normal operating hours, supervision may be required before and after class hours when students are known to congregate on school ground."

In one such case, *Titus v. Lindberg* 228 1A. 2d 65 (N.J., 1967), the administrator was found to be liable for a student injury occurring on school grounds before school because he knew that students arrived on the grounds before the doors were opened; he was present on the campus when they were; he had established no rules for student conduct outside the building, nor had he provided for supervision of the students. The court found that he had a reasonable duty to provide such supervision when he knew students were on the property and that students were there as a regular practice.

The *Titus* case illustrates the dilemma in which school administrators may find themselves. If a parent drops a student off at the school at 6:30 a.m. and the school opens at 7:00 a.m., is the administrator responsible for the student? How does the administrator provide for supervision? Should supervision be afforded? As Chapter IV discusses, there are no easy answers to the problem of supervision of students before school, after school, and while waiting for activities to begin. But the administrator and the school must develop some policy and/or procedures to deal with the reality that students will be present at unauthorized times.

It is important to keep in mind that the court will look at the reasonable nature of the administrator's behavior. Is it reasonable to expect that an administrator will provide for the supervision of students on school grounds no matter how early they arrive and how late they stay? Probably no court would expect an administrator to be present at 6:00 a.m.; however, the court will expect some policy or statement as to when students may arrive on campus, what rules they are to follow, and what kind of supervision will be provided.

Common sense also has to prevail. If the administrator arrives at school thirty minutes before the doors open and a child is standing outside in sub-zero weather, the reasonable person would bring the child indoors. Gatti and Gatti, (1983, p. 246) state, "All people owe all other people the 'duty' of not subjecting them to an unreasonable risk or harm." A court might well find in a situation where a child is standing outside in freezing weather that the administrator had a duty to protect the child from harm.

The second element involved in negligence is violation of duty. Negligence cannot exist if the administrator or teacher has not violated a duty. Courts expect that accidents and spontaneous actions can occur. If a teacher is properly supervising a playground, and one child picks up a rock and throws it and so injures another child, the teacher cannot be held liable. However, if a teacher who is responsible for the supervision of the playground were to allow rock-throwing to continue without attempting to stop it and a student were injured, the teacher would probably be held liable. Similarly, a teacher who leaves a classroom unattended in order to take a coffee break will generally be held to have violated a duty. But if it can be demonstrated that teachers have, as a general practice, taken coffee breaks and left classes unattended, and, because of the inattention or inaction of the principal, nothing was done about the situation, the principal will be held equally, if not more, liable, than the teacher.

The third requirement of negligence is that the violation of duty must be the proximate cause of the injury: "The question usually asked is, 'did the educator's action or inaction' have a material and immediate effect in producing the injury?" (Permuth, Mawdsley and Daly, 1981, p. 13). In other words, would the injury have occurred if proper supervision had been present? The court or jury has to decide whether proper supervision could have prevented the injury and, in so deciding, the court has to look at the facts of each individual case. Valente (1980) commented on the concept of proximate cause:

> To be proximate, a cause need not be the immediate, or even the primary cause of injury, but it must be a *material and substantial* factor in producing the harm, 'but for' which the harm would not have occurred. (p. 351)

The tragic case of *Levandoski v. Jackson City School District* 328 So. 2d 339 (Minn. 1976) illustrates the validity of Valente's comments. In this case, the principal and teacher failed to report that a thirteen year old girl was missing from school. The child was later found murdered. The child's mother filed suit against the school district and alleged that, if the child's absence had been reported, the murder would not have happened. However, the court found that no evidence existed to show that if the teacher and principal had properly and promptly reported the child's absence, the murder could have been prevented. One should not draw the conclusion that carelessness in reporting absences is not a serious matter; it certainly seems possible that another court with the same or slightly different facts might have reached another conclusion. The *Levandoski* court simply found that the principal's and the teacher's violation of duty was not the proximate cause of the injury which, in this case, was death.

The case of *Smith v. Archbishop of St. Louis* 632 S.W. 2d 516 (Mo. Ct. App. 1982), which involved a Catholic school, illustrates the concept of proximate cause. In this case, a second grade teacher kept a lighted candle on her desk every morning during May in honor of the Mother of God. She gave no special instructions to the students regarding the danger of a lighted candle. One day, a school play was to be held in which the plaintiff played the part of a bird and for which she had a costume partially composed of crepe paper. While the teacher was helping some students in another part of the classroom, the plaintiff's costume caught fire. The teacher had difficulty putting out the flames, and the child sustained facial and upper body burns such that during the five years the litigation was in process, she was subjected to several operations and to painful treatments. It was demonstrated that she had sustained psychological as well as physical damage and that the likelihood was that she would continue to experience psychological problems throughout her lifetime. The trial court had awarded the child $1,250,000 damages. The appellate court upheld the award and the finding of negligent supervision against the archdiocese. This case demonstrates the liability that can accrue to a Catholic school and to a diocese because of the negligence of a teacher or an administrator.

The *Smith* case also illustrates the concept of foreseeability. The plaintiff did not have to prove that the defendant could foresee that a particular injury (plaintiff's costume catching fire) had to occur; the plaintiff had to establish that a reasonable person would have foreseen the injuries that could result from having an unattended lighted candle in a second grade classroom when no safety instructions had been given to the students.

In determining whether a teacher's behavior was reasonable, the court might ask the following questions. (1) Has the teacher given the students clear instructions as to how to behave in his or her absence? (2) Is the teacher absent a reasonable length of time? Five minutes seem reasonable; a thirty minute absence during which a teacher took a coffee break, made a phone call, or copied papers would probably not be considered reasonable.

In determining whether the principal would be liable for accidents occurring during a teacher's absence, the court might pose these questions: (1) Has the principal developed a clear policy for teachers who need to leave classrooms? (2) Has the principal implemented the policy? (3) Has he or she supervised teachers to make sure that they are following the policy?

From the above discussion, it should be apparent that negligence is a difficult concept to understand fully and that it is often difficult to predict what a court will determine to be proximate cause in any particular allegation of negligence.

The fourth element necessary for a finding of negligence is injury. No matter how irresponsible the behavior of a teacher or administrator, there is no negligence if there is no injury. If a teacher leaves twenty first-graders unsupervised near a lake and no one is injured, there can be no finding of negligence and, hence, no tort. Any reasonable person, though, can see that no one in authority should take risks that may result in injury.

Most negligence cases occur in the classroom because that is where students and teachers spend most of their time. However, there are other areas that are potentially more dangerous than the classroom and, hence, a greater standard of care will be expected from teachers and administrators.

Shop and lab classes contain greater potential for injury and cases indicate that courts expect teachers to exercise greater caution than they would in ordinary classrooms. Teachers and administrators are further expected to maintain equipment in working order and to keep the area free of unnecessary hazards. It is also expected that students will be given safety instructions regarding the use of potentially dangerous equipment. In *Station V. Travelers Insurance Co.*, 292 So. 2d 289 (La. Ct. App. 1974), school officials were found to be negligent when injury resulted from the use of a science lab burner that was known to be defective.

Athletics present another hazard, probably one of the most serious. Even if every possible precaution were taken, the possibility for student injury during athletics is very high. Administrators (who very often are content to let athletic directors and coaches worry about athletic programs) have very real duties to insure that: competent, properly trained personnel serve as coaches for teams; that clear procedures are followed when accidents occur; that there is no delay in seeking medical attention (when even the slightest possibility exists that medical help might be needed); and that equipment and playing areas are as hazard-free as possible.

The younger the child, the greater will be the responsibility of the educator. It might be acceptable to leave a group of high school seniors alone for ten minutes in a math class when it would not be acceptable to leave a group of first graders alone. It is reasonable to expect that fifteen-year-olds of average intelligence could observe traffic signals when they are crossing a street. It would not be reasonable to expect mentally handicapped fifteen-year-olds to be responsible for crossing the street.

In developing and implementing policies for supervision, the educator must keep in mind the reasonableness standards and ask, "Is this what one would expect a reasonable person in a similar situation to do?" No one expects a principal or teacher to think of every possible situation that might occur. A court would not necessarily consider it unreasonable if a school did not have a rule prohibiting throwing chairs; the court would expect, though, that there would be some sort of rule encompassing the possibility of such an activity, for example, "Students are not to throw objects." No one can foresee everything that might happen, but reasonable persons can assume that certain situations are potentially dangerous. The teacher in the *Smith* case should have foreseen that second graders might be injured by an open flame.

The best defense for an administrator in a negligence suit is the development of reasonable policies and rules for the safety of those entrusted to his or her care. The reasonable administrator is one who supervises teachers and others in their implementation of rules.

Corporal Punishment

Corporal punishment may be defined as any physical contact that could be construed as punitive. In 1977 the Supreme Court declared that school children had no constitutional protection against corporal punishment (*Ingraham v. Wright* 430 U.S. 65).

There appears, however, to be a trend, particularly in the wake of growing awareness of child abuse, away from corporal punishment in all schools. Although corporal punishment is still allowed by statute in the majority of states, many states have legislation pending which would outlaw corporal punishment in all schools, whether public or nonpublic.

Generally, if corporal punishment is to be used, the following guidelines should be observed:

(1) corporal punishment should be permitted by the state;
(2) punishment should be for the correction of the child;
(3) punishment should not leave permanent or lasting injury;
(4) punishment must be administered with an appropriate instrument; and
(5) the number of "blows" should probably not exceed three.

Catholic school personnel are not immune to civil tort cases or criminal charges of assault and battery if corporal punishment results in injuries to the student.

Catholic school administrators, like public school officials, might be well advised to require other means of discipline than physical ones, both from the standpoint of avoiding lawsuits and from the standpoints of one's school philosophy and good psychology.

Search and Seizure

In 1985 the Supreme Court heard the case of *New Jersey v. T.L.O.* 105 S.Ct. 733, involving an administrative search of a student's purse which resulted in the student's being charged with possession of marijuana. The court ruled that public school officials need have only reasonable, rather than probable, cause to search students. Public school search and seizure cases generally distinguish between probable and reasonable cause. Probable cause is a stricter standard than reasonable cause and will be held to exist when an administrator has reliable knowledge about the whereabouts of illegal or dangerous material on campus. Reasonable cause might include anonymous phone calls or rumors.

Catholic school officials, although not bound to observe even the reasonable cause standard, should, nonetheless, have some kind of policy for searching students and/or seizing their possessions. Searching a student should require more cause than searching a locker.

Catholic school educators could be subject to tort suits if harm is alleged to have been done to a student because of an unreasonable search: "Searches of students will have to be conducted according to the 'reasonable person' doctrine of tort law; that test includes not only the manner of search, but the justification for the search in the first place" (Permuth, Mawdsley and Daly, 1981, p. 65). Catholic school officials could be charged with the torts of assault and battery and/or invasion of privacy.

Defamation

Defamation is the violation of a person's liberty interest or right to reputation. *Black's Law Dictionary* defines defamation as: "Includes both libel [what is written] and slander [what is spoken]. Defamation is that which tends to injure the reputation; to diminish the esteem, respect, goodwill or confidence in which the plaintiff is held, or to excite adverse, derogatory or unpleasant feelings or opinions against him. . . " (p. 375).

The potential for defamation to be alleged certainly exists in administrators' relationships with students and with teachers. It is important that administrators be factual in their comments, whether written or oral, about the conduct of either teachers or students.

Several authors have pointed out that the truth is not always the best defense, since truthful statements can be defamatory (Gatti and Gatti, 1983). The truth may be a valid defense only if the statement was made without malice and to another person who has the right to know.

When making statements or writing entries in records, an administrator should seek to restrict statements to pertinent facts. Comments should be objective, behaviorally-oriented and verifiable.

Student records, in accordance with the provisions of the *Buckley Amendment*, should be made available only to parents and to staff who have a need for access to such information.

Personnel records should contain only items that have been shared with the employee and no one other than the employee. The administration of the school should have access to those records. If personnel records are sent to another employer, the school administrator should be sure that a written release is obtained from the employee.

Child Abuse/Neglect/Sexual Abuse Reporting

All fifty states have laws requiring educational personnel who have reason to believe that a child is being abused or neglected to report that suspicion to the appropriate authority. Failure to report can result in certain sanctions. Administrators must insure that faculty and staff receive some instruction regarding the indicators of neglect and abuse and that school personnel receive clear directions as to the procedure for reporting such situations.

An administrator may wish to make all reports personally; such a procedure is acceptable and will insure that the principal knows all such reports. However, teachers must know that, if for some reason, a principal does not wish to make a report, the teacher is responsible for doing so.

Many legal experts will point out that it is not the educator's responsibility to determine if abuse or neglect has occurred; that duty belongs to the police and social services departments. It is, however, the clear responsibility of school personnel to report any situations that raise reasonable suspicions in their minds.

Non-traditional Families

The rights of non-custodial parents have been discussed in Chapter II. It is important that administrators know who has legal custody and what, if any, access to a child a non-custodial parent has.

School officials also need to understand that other relatives have no right of access to a student, unless that right of access is granted by the custodial parent or guardian. Catholic school principals must implement clear policies and keep accurate records indicating who, besides parents, may call for a student at school or otherwise have contact with that individual. When in doubt, an administrator should contact the custodial parent immediately.

A Final Thought

The development of the law as it affects Catholic schools has been much slower than the development of public school law. However, the last decade has seen a great increase in the number of lawsuits brought against Catholic schools. Case law indicates that courts will exercise jurisdiction over those aspects of a Catholic school's operation that are not religious in nature.

Knowledge of school law can help Catholic school personnel be more effective administrators, and at the same time, avoid lawsuits. The principles of nonpublic school law are based on the common law standard of fairness. The Gospel, as well as the law, demands that Catholic school administrators, seeking to be faithful to the mission and philosophy of their schools, pursue knowledge of the law. The courts have indicated that Catholic schools will be held to a standard of fundamental reasonableness. It is by that standard, and by the requirements of the Gospel, that Catholic school administrators should seek to judge their actions, whether or not those actions are ever tested in a court of law.

GLOSSARY OF TERMS

Board

A board (committee/council/commission) is a body whose members are selected or elected to participate in decision-making in education at the diocesan, regional, inter-parish or parish level.

> *Board with Limited Jurisdiction* A board with limited jurisdiction has power limited to certain areas of educational concern. It has final but not total jurisdiction.

> *Consultative Board* A consultative board is one which cooperates in the policy-making process by formulating and adapting but never enacting policy. (CACE/NABE, p. 59).

Collegiality

Collegiality is a sharing of responsibility and authority. In the Catholic Church, bishops have the highest authority within a diocese. Powers may be delegated to other parties, such as boards.

Common Law

Common law is that law not created by a legislature. It includes principles of action based on long-established standards of reasonable conduct and on court judgments affirming such standards. It is sometimes called "judge-made law."

Compelling State Interest

Compelling state interest is the overwhelming or serious need for governmental action. The government is said to have a compelling state interest in anti-discrimination legislation or the equal treatment of all citizens.

Contract

A contract is an agreement between two parties. The essentials of a contract are: (1) mutual assent (2) by legally competent parties (3) for consideration (4) to subject matter that is legal and (5) in a form of agreement that is legal.

Consensus

As distinguished form majority rule, consensus is a model of decision-making in which a board seeks to arrive at a decision that all members can agree to support.

Defamation

Defamation is communication that injures the reputation of another without good reason. Defamation can be either spoken (slander) or written (libel).

Due Process

Due process is fundamental fairness under the law. There are two types:

Substantive Due Process: "The constitutional guarantee that no person shall be arbitrarily deprived of his life,liberty or property; the essence of substantive due process is protection from arbitrary unreasonable action" (Black, p. 1281). Substantive due process concerns *what* is done as distinguished from *how* it is done (procedural due process).

Procedural Due Process: how the process of depriving someone of something is carried out; *how it is done.* The minimum requirements of constitutional due process are *notice* and a *hearing* before an *impartial tribunal.*

Executive Session
An executive session is a closed meeting to which only members of the board are admitted. If the board is discussing the evaluation of the job performance of a board member, such as the principal, that person may be asked to leave the meeting during the discussion.

Fiduciary
A fiduciary is one who has accepted the responsibility for the care of people or property.

Foreseeability
Foreseeability is "the reasonable anticipation that harm or injury is likely result of acts or omission" (Black, p. 584). It is not necessary that a person anticipate that a specific injury might result from an action, but only that danger or harm in general might result.

Judicial Restraint
Judicial restraint is the doctrine that courts will not interfere in decisions made by professionals.

Landmark Court Decisions
Landmark court decisions are decisions of major importance. These decisions are often used as part of the judicial reasoning in later decisions.

Negligence
Negligence is the absence of the degree of care which a reasonable person would be expected to use in a given situation.

Policy
A policy is a guide for discretionary action. (CACE/NABE, p. 6l). Policy states *what* is to be done, not *how* it is to be done.

Proximate Cause
Proximate cause is a contributing factor to an injury. The injury was a result or reasonably foreseeable outcome

Glossary of Terms

of the action or inaction said to be the proximate cause.

Public Benefit Theory
The theory which states that an institution which performs a public benefit is a state agent. This theory has been generally rejected by the courts.

State Action
State action is the presence of the government in an activity to such a degree that the activity may be considered to be that of the government.

Subsidiarity
Subsidiarity is the principle that problems should be solved at the lowest possible level. Thus, if there is a complaint against a teacher, the teacher must be confronted before the principal is approached.

Tenure
Tenure is an expectation of continuing employment.

De Facto Tenure: De facto tenure is an expectation *in fact* that employment will continue, in the absence of a formal tenure policy. *De facto* tenure can result from past practices of an employer or from length of employment.

Tort
A tort is a civil or private wrong as distinguished from a crime.

BIBLIOGRAPHY

Alexander, Kern. *School law.* St. Paul: West, 1980.

Black, Henry Campbell. *Black's law dictionary.* (5th ed.). St. Paul: West.

Bloch V. Hillel Torah North Suburban Day School, 438 N.E. 2d 976 L981).

Board of Regents v. Roth, 408 U.S. 564, 92 S. Ct. 2701 (1972).

Bob Jones University v. United States, 103 S. Ct. 2017 (1983).

Bright v. Isenbarger, 314 F. Supp. 1382 (1970).

Chief Administrators of Catholic Education/National Association of Boards of Education. (J. Stephen O'Brien, ed.) *A Primer on Eductional Governance in the Catholic Church.* Washington, DC: National Catholic Educational Association, 1987.

Clear, Delbert and Martha Bagley. "Coaching athletics: a tort just waiting for a judgment?" *Nolpe School Law Journal,* 10 (2), 184-92, 1982.

Delon, Floyd G. and Robert E Bartman. "Employees." In Philip K. Piele (Ed.). *The yearbook of school law* (pp.45-130). Topeka: National Organization on Legal Problems of Education, 1979

Dixon v. Alabama State B.O.E., 294 F. 2d 150, cert. den. 368 U.S. 930 (1961).

Dolter v. Wahlert, 483 F. Supp. 266 (n.D. Iowa 1980).

Bibliography

Echols, Robert M., Jr. and Steven F. Casey. "Comments: the right to counsel in disciplinary proceedings in public and private educational institutions." *Cumberland Law Review 9,* 751-766, (1979).

Gatti, Richard D. and Daniel J. Gatti. *New Encyclopedic Dictionary of School Law.* West Nyack, NY: Parker, 1983

Geraci v. St. Xavier High School, 13 Ohio Op. 3d 146 (Ohio, 1978).

Goss v. Lopez, 419 U.S. 565 (1975).

Ingraham v. Wright, 430 U.S. 65 (1977).

LaMorte, Michael W. "Rights and responsibilities in light of social contract theory." *Educational Administration Quarterly, 13,* pp. 31-48, (1977, Fall).

Levandowski v. Jackson City School District, 328 So. 2d 339 (Minn. 1976).

National Labor Relations Board v. Catholic Bishop of Chicago, 440 U.S. 490 (1979).

Permuth, Steve, et al. *The law, the student and the Catholic school.* Washington, D.C.: National Catholic Educational Association, 1981.

Perry v. Sindermann, 408 U.S. 593 (1972).

Phay, Robert E. *The Law of Procedures in Student Suspensions and Expulsions.* Topeka: NOLPE (ERIC N. EA 009345), 1977.

Pierce v. the Society of Sisters, 268 U.S. 510 (1925).

Reardon et al. v. LeMoyne et al., 454 A. 2d 428 (N.H. 1982).

Rendell-Baker v. Kohn, 102 S. Ct. 2764 (1982).

Reutter, E.E., Jr. "The Courts and Student Conduct." Topeka, KS: NOLPE (ERIC Document Reproduction Service No. ED 006 406), 1977.

Seavey, Warren A. "Dismissal of students: due process." *Harvard Law Review, 70,* 1406-1410, 1957.

Shaughnessy, Mary Angela. *School Law Primer: A Guide for Board Members in Catholic Schools.* Washington, D.C.:

National Catholic Educational Association, 1988.

Smith v. Archbishop of St. Louis, 632 S.W. 2d 516 (Mo. Ct. App. 1982).

Station v. Travelers Insurance Co., 292 So. 2d 289 (La. Ct. App. 1974).

Steeber v. Benilde— St. Margaret's High School, (No. D.C. 739378, Hennepin County, Minnesota, 1978).

Stern, Ralph D. "The principal and tort liability." In R. D. Stern (Ed.). *The school principal and the law* (pp. 205-220), 1978.

Tinker v. Des Moines Independent Community School District et al., 393 U.S. 503 (1969).

Titus v. Lindberg, 228 A. 2d 65 (N.J., 1967).

Valente, William D. *Law in the schools*. Columbus: Merrill, 1980.

Weithoff v. St. Veronica School, 210 N.W. 2d 108 (Mich. 1973).

Wisch v. Sanford School, Inc., 420 F. Supp. 1310 (1976).

Wright, Charles A. "The constitution on the campus." *Vanderbilt Law Review*, 22, 1027-1088, 1969.

INDEX